The Ultimate
Air Fryer
Cookbook

UK 2023

1200 Days Simple, Effortless and Mouthwatering Air Fryer
Recipes for Your Whole Family and Friends (2023 Edition)

Santina Crooks

Table of Contents

♦ Chapter 4 Fish and Seafood 25

♦ Chapter 5 Beef, Pork, and Lamb 34

♦ Chapter 6 Vegetables and Sides 44

◆ Chapter 7 Snacks and Appetisers 49

◆ Chapter 8 Desserts 57

◆ Chapter 9 Pizzas, Wraps, and Sandwiches 65

INTRODUCTION

You may have heard of the air fryer from your best friend, your mom, or your culinary curiosity. It's turned every one from being afraid to cook at home to loving cooking. Dieters rejoice at how they can make crispy foods without those pesky oils. And those in a hurry love how fast it cooks.

I know I loved mine when I bought it. But, at first, I wondered if it could meet the hype. There are so many appliances that are big fads for a bit. But, these appliances that rule the world go out of style when all is said and done. Yet, for the air fryer, there's a reason why people still love it.

It's one of the most convenient modern appliances, and every kitchen should have one of these, if only for the convenience of cooking.

It turned me from a guy who liked to eat out to someone who spends time cooking his food and saving money at home. Plus, the foods taste better. So I was inspired to try out new recipes, make my own twists on them, and list some of my favorites, which I'm doing in this cookbook.

This cookbook combines several of my favorite recipes in one comprehensive guide. I have recipes for all times of the day, family sizes, and skill levels. For example, you can learn how to make fried chicken to perfection or about the many surprises that air fryers can offer you.

You can do a lot more than fry your favorite foods. Since the air fryer is a convection oven, you can use it for baking foods, reheating them, and doing almost everything your oven can. Since you can control your portions, it also means that you won't be spending time worrying about leftovers or overeating.

Best of all, this cookbook makes cooking easy and it provides easy-to-follow instructions, and recipes with simple ingredients. Chances are, you may have most of the ingredients at home. I bet the nearest store will have them if you don't.

So let's look at my favorite recipes.

Chapter 1 Breakfasts

Chapter 1 Breakfasts

Chimichanga Breakfast Burrito

Prep time: 10 minutes | Cook time: 10 minutes | Serves 2

2 large (10- to 12-inch) flour tortillas	4 corn tortilla chips, crushed
120 ml canned refried beans (pinto or black work equally well)	120 ml grated chili cheese
	12 pickled jalapeño slices
	1 tablespoon vegetable oil
4 large eggs, cooked scrambled	Guacamole, salsa, and sour cream, for serving (optional)

Place the tortillas on a work surface and divide the refried beans between them, spreading them in a rough rectangle in the center of the tortillas. Top the beans with the scrambled eggs, crushed chips, cheese, and jalapeños. Fold one side over the fillings, then fold in each short side and roll up the rest of the way like a burrito. Brush the outside of the burritos with the oil, then transfer to the air fryer, seam-side down. Air fry at 176°C until the tortillas are browned and crisp and the filling is warm throughout, about 10 minutes. Transfer the chimichangas to plates and serve warm with guacamole, salsa, and sour cream, if you like.

Breakfast Cobbler

Prep time: 20 minutes | Cook time: 30 minutes | Serves 4

Filling:	Biscuits:
280 g sausage meat, crumbled	3 large egg whites
60 ml minced onions	180 ml blanched almond flour
2 cloves garlic, minced	1 teaspoon baking powder
½ teaspoon fine sea salt	¼ teaspoon fine sea salt
½ teaspoon ground black pepper	2½ tablespoons very cold unsalted butter, cut into ¼-inch pieces
1 (230 g) package cream cheese (or cream cheese style spread for dairy-free), softened	
	Fresh thyme leaves, for garnish
180 ml beef or chicken stock	

Preheat the air fryer to 204°C. Place the sausage, onions, and garlic in a pie pan. Using your hands, break up the sausage into small pieces and spread it evenly throughout the pie pan. Season with the salt and pepper. Place the pan in the air fryer and bake for 5 minutes. While the sausage cooks, place the cream cheese and stock in a food processor or blender and purée until smooth. Remove the pork from the air fryer and use a fork or metal spatula to crumble it more. Pour the cream cheese mixture into the sausage and stir to combine. Set aside. Make the biscuits: Place the egg whites in a medium-sized mixing bowl or the bowl of a stand mixer and whip with a hand mixer or stand mixer until stiff peaks form. In a separate medium-sized bowl, whisk together the almond flour, baking powder, and salt, then cut in the butter. When you are done, the mixture should still have chunks of butter. Gently fold the flour mixture into the egg whites with a rubber spatula. Use a large spoon or ice cream scoop to scoop the dough into 4 equal-sized biscuits, making sure the butter is evenly distributed. Place the biscuits on top of the sausage and cook in the air fryer for 5 minutes, then turn the heat down to 164°C and bake for another 17 to 20 minutes, until the biscuits are golden brown. Serve garnished with fresh thyme leaves. Store leftovers in an airtight container in the refrigerator for up to 3 days. Reheat in a preheated 176°C air fryer for 5 minutes, or until warmed through.

Parmesan Ranch Risotto

Prep time: 10 minutes | Cook time: 30 minutes | Serves 2

1 tablespoon olive oil	180 ml Arborio rice
1 clove garlic, minced	475 ml chicken stock, boiling
1 tablespoon unsalted butter	120 ml Parmesan cheese, grated
1 onion, diced	

Preheat the air fryer to 200°C. Grease a round baking tin with olive oil and stir in the garlic, butter, and onion. Transfer the tin to the air fryer and bake for 4 minutes. Add the rice and bake for 4 more minutes. Turn the air fryer to 160°C and pour in the chicken stock. Cover and bake for 22 minutes. Scatter with cheese and serve.

Cinnamon Rolls

Prep time: 10 minutes | Cook time: 20 minutes | Makes 12 rolls

600 ml shredded Mozzarella cheese	½ teaspoon vanilla extract
	120 ml icing sugar-style sweetener
60 g cream cheese, softened	
235 ml blanched finely ground almond flour	1 tablespoon ground cinnamon

In a large microwave-safe bowl, combine Mozzarella cheese, cream cheese, and flour. Microwave the mixture on high 90 seconds until cheese is melted. Add vanilla extract and sweetener, and mix 2 minutes until a dough forms. Once the dough is cool enough to work with your hands, about 2 minutes, spread it out into a 12 × 4-inch rectangle on ungreased parchment paper. Evenly sprinkle dough with cinnamon. Starting at the long side of the dough, roll lengthwise to form a log. Slice the log into twelve even pieces. Divide rolls between two ungreased round nonstick baking dishes. Place one dish into air fryer basket. Adjust the temperature to 192°C and bake for 10 minutes. Cinnamon rolls will be done when golden around the edges and mostly firm. Repeat with second dish. Allow rolls to cool in dishes 10 minutes before serving.

Italian Egg Cups

Prep time: 5 minutes | Cook time: 10 minutes | Serves 4

Olive oil
235 ml marinara sauce
4 eggs
4 tablespoons shredded
Mozzarella cheese

4 teaspoons grated Parmesan
cheese
Salt and freshly ground black
pepper, to taste
Chopped fresh basil, for garnish

Lightly spray 4 individual ramekins with olive oil. Pour 60 ml marinara sauce into each ramekin. Crack one egg into each ramekin on top of the marinara sauce. Sprinkle 1 tablespoon of Mozzarella and 1 tablespoon of Parmesan on top of each egg. Season with salt and pepper. Cover each ramekin with aluminum foil. Place two of the ramekins in the air fryer basket. Air fry at 176ºC for 5 minutes and remove the aluminum foil. Air fry until the top is lightly browned and the egg white is cooked, another 2 to 4 minutes. If you prefer the yolk to be firmer, cook for 3 to 5 more minutes. Repeat with the remaining two ramekins. Garnish with basil and serve.

Sausage Stuffed Peppers

Prep time: 15 minutes | Cook time: 15 minutes | Serves 4

230 g spicy pork sausage meat,
removed from casings
4 large eggs
110 g full-fat cream cheese,
softened
60 ml tinned diced tomatoes,

drained
4 green peppers
8 tablespoons shredded chilli
cheese
120 ml full-fat sour cream

In a medium skillet over medium heat, crumble and brown the sausage meat until no pink remains. Remove sausage and drain the fat from the pan. Crack eggs into the pan, scramble, and cook until no longer runny. Place cooked sausage in a large bowl and fold in cream cheese. Mix in diced tomatoes. Gently fold in eggs. Cut a 4-inch to 5-inch slit in the top of each pepper, removing the seeds and white membrane with a small knife. Separate the filling into four servings and spoon carefully into each pepper. Top each with 2 tablespoons cheese. Place each pepper into the air fryer basket. Adjust the temperature to 176ºC and set the timer for 15 minutes. Peppers will be soft and cheese will be browned when ready. Serve immediately with sour cream on top.

Tomato and Mozzarella Bruschetta

Prep time: 5 minutes | Cook time: 4 minutes | Serves 1

6 small loaf slices
120 ml tomatoes, finely chopped
85 g Mozzarella cheese, grated

1 tablespoon fresh basil,
chopped
1 tablespoon olive oil

Preheat the air fryer to 176ºC. Put the loaf slices inside the air fryer and air fry for about 3 minutes. Add the tomato, Mozzarella, basil, and olive oil on top. Air fry for an additional minute before serving.

Cajun Breakfast Sausage

Prep time: 10 minutes | Cook time: 15 to 20 minutes | Serves 8

680 g 85% lean turkey mince
3 cloves garlic, finely chopped
¼ onion, grated
1 teaspoon Tabasco sauce

1 teaspoon Cajun seasoning
1 teaspoon dried thyme
½ teaspoon paprika
½ teaspoon cayenne

Preheat the air fryer to 188ºC. In a large bowl, combine the turkey, garlic, onion, Tabasco, Cajun seasoning, thyme, paprika, and cayenne. Mix with clean hands until thoroughly combined. Shape into 16 patties, about ½ inch thick. (Wet your hands slightly if you find the sausage too sticky to handle.) Working in batches if necessary, arrange the patties in a single layer in the air fryer basket. Pausing halfway through the cooking time to flip the patties, air fry for 15 to 20 minutes until a thermometer inserted into the thickest portion registers 74ºC.

Portobello Eggs Benedict

Prep time: 10 minutes | Cook time: 10 to 14 minutes | Serves 2

1 tablespoon olive oil
2 cloves garlic, minced
¼ teaspoon dried thyme
2 portobello mushrooms, stems
removed and gills scraped out
2 plum tomatoes, halved
lengthwise
Salt and freshly ground black

pepper, to taste
2 large eggs
2 tablespoons grated Pecorino
Romano cheese
1 tablespoon chopped fresh
parsley, for garnish
1 teaspoon truffle oil (optional)

Preheat the air fryer to 204ºC. In a small bowl, combine the olive oil, garlic, and thyme. Brush the mixture over the mushrooms and tomatoes until thoroughly coated. Season to taste with salt and freshly ground black pepper. Arrange the vegetables, cut side up, in the air fryer basket. Crack an egg into the center of each mushroom and sprinkle with cheese. Air fry for 10 to 14 minutes until the vegetables are tender and the whites are firm. When cool enough to handle, coarsely chop the tomatoes and place on top of the eggs. Scatter parsley on top and drizzle with truffle oil, if desired, just before serving.

Gold Avocado

Prep time: 5 minutes | Cook time: 6 minutes | Serves 4

2 large avocados, sliced
¼ teaspoon paprika
Salt and ground black pepper, to
taste

120 ml flour
2 eggs, beaten
235 ml bread crumbs

Preheat the air fryer to 204ºC. Sprinkle paprika, salt and pepper on the slices of avocado. Lightly coat the avocados with flour. Dredge them in the eggs, before covering with bread crumbs. Transfer to the air fryer and air fry for 6 minutes. Serve warm.

White Bean–Oat Waffles

Prep time: 10 minutes | Cook time: 20 minutes | Serves 2

1 large egg white
2 tablespoons finely ground flaxseed
120 ml water
¼ teaspoon salt
1 teaspoon vanilla extract
120 ml cannellini beans, drained

and rinsed
1 teaspoon coconut oil
1 teaspoon liquid sweetener
120 ml old-fashioned rolled oats
Extra-virgin olive oil cooking spray

In a blender, combine the egg white, flaxseed, water, salt, vanilla, cannellini beans, coconut oil, and sweetener. Blend on high for 90 seconds. Add the oats. Blend for 1 minute more. Preheat the waffle iron. The batter will thicken to the correct consistency while the waffle iron preheats. Spray the heated waffle iron with cooking spray. Add 180 ml batter. Close the waffle iron. Cook for 6 to 8 minutes, or until done. Repeated with the remaining batter. Serve hot, with your favorite sugar-free topping.

Potatoes Lyonnaise

Prep time: 10 minutes | Cook time: 31 minutes | Serves 4

1 sweet/mild onion, sliced
1 teaspoon butter, melted
1 teaspoon brown sugar
2 large white potatoes (about 450 g in total), sliced ½-inch

thick
1 tablespoon vegetable oil
Salt and freshly ground black pepper, to taste

Preheat the air fryer to 188ºC. Toss the sliced onions, melted butter and brown sugar together in the air fryer basket. Air fry for 8 minutes, shaking the basket occasionally to help the onions cook evenly. While the onions are cooking, bring a saucepan of salted water to a boil on the stovetop. Par-cook the potatoes in boiling water for 3 minutes. Drain the potatoes and pat them dry with a clean kitchen towel. Add the potatoes to the onions in the air fryer basket and drizzle with vegetable oil. Toss to coat the potatoes with the oil and season with salt and freshly ground black pepper. Increase the air fryer temperature to 204ºC and air fry for 20 minutes, tossing the vegetables a few times during the cooking time to help the potatoes brown evenly. Season with salt and freshly ground black pepper and serve warm.

All-in-One Toast

Prep time: 10 minutes | Cook time: 10 minutes | Serves 1

1 strip bacon, diced
1 slice 1-inch thick bread
1 egg
Salt and freshly ground black

pepper, to taste
60 ml grated Monterey Jack or Chedday cheese

Preheat the air fryer to 204ºC. Air fry the bacon for 3 minutes, shaking the basket once or twice while it cooks. Remove the bacon to a paper towel lined plate and set aside. Use a sharp paring knife to score a large circle in the middle of the slice of bread, cutting halfway through, but not all the way through to the cutting board. Press down on the circle in the center of the bread slice to create an indentation. Transfer the slice of bread, hole side up, to the air fryer basket. Crack the egg into the center of the bread, and season with salt and pepper. Adjust the air fryer temperature to 192ºC and air fry for 5 minutes. Sprinkle the grated cheese around the edges of the bread, leaving the center of the yolk uncovered, and top with the cooked bacon. Press the cheese and bacon into the bread lightly to help anchor it to the bread and prevent it from blowing around in the air fryer. Air fry for one or two more minutes, just to melt the cheese and finish cooking the egg. Serve immediately.

Pizza Eggs

Prep time: 5 minutes | Cook time: 10 minutes | Serves 2

235 ml shredded Mozzarella cheese
7 slices pepperoni, chopped
1 large egg, whisked

¼ teaspoon dried oregano
¼ teaspoon dried parsley
¼ teaspoon garlic powder
¼ teaspoon salt

Place Mozzarella in a single layer on the bottom of an ungreased round nonstick baking dish. Scatter pepperoni over cheese, then pour egg evenly around baking dish. Sprinkle with remaining ingredients and place into air fryer basket. Adjust the temperature to 166ºC and bake for 10 minutes. When cheese is brown and egg is set, dish will be done. Let cool in dish 5 minutes before serving.

Hearty Blueberry Oatmeal

Prep time: 10 minutes | Cook time: 25 minutes | Serves 6

350 ml quick oats
1¼ teaspoons ground cinnamon, divided
½ teaspoon baking powder
Pinch salt
235 ml unsweetened vanilla almond milk
60 ml honey

1 teaspoon vanilla extract
1 egg, beaten
475 ml blueberries
Olive oil
1½ teaspoons sugar, divided
6 tablespoons low-fat whipped topping (optional)

In a large bowl, mix together the oats, 1 teaspoon of cinnamon, baking powder, and salt. In a medium bowl, whisk together the almond milk, honey, vanilla and egg. Pour the liquid ingredients into the oats mixture and stir to combine. Fold in the blueberries. Lightly spray a baking pan with oil. Add half the blueberry mixture to the pan. Sprinkle ⅛ teaspoon of cinnamon and ½ teaspoon sugar over the top. Cover the pan with aluminum foil and place gently in the air fryer basket. Air fry at 182ºC for 20 minutes. Remove the foil and air fry for an additional 5 minutes. Transfer the mixture to a shallow bowl. Repeat with the remaining blueberry mixture, ½ teaspoon of sugar, and ⅛ teaspoon of cinnamon. 1To serve, spoon into bowls and top with whipped topping.

Easy Sausage Pizza

Prep time: 10 minutes | Cook time: 6 minutes | Serves 4

2 tablespoons ketchup
1 pitta bread
80 ml sausage meat

230 g Mozzarella cheese
1 teaspoon garlic powder
1 tablespoon olive oil

Preheat the air fryer to 172°C. Spread the ketchup over the pitta bread. Top with the sausage meat and cheese. Sprinkle with the garlic powder and olive oil. Put the pizza in the air fryer basket and bake for 6 minutes. Serve warm.

Easy Buttermilk Biscuits

Prep time: 5 minutes | Cook time: 18 minutes | Makes 16 biscuits

600 ml plain flour
1 tablespoon baking powder
1 teaspoon coarse or flaky salt
1 teaspoon sugar

½ teaspoon baking soda
8 tablespoons (1 stick) unsalted butter, at room temperature
235 ml buttermilk, chilled

Stir together the flour, baking powder, salt, sugar, and baking powder in a large bowl. Add the butter and stir to mix well. Pour in the buttermilk and stir with a rubber spatula just until incorporated. Place the dough onto a lightly floured surface and roll the dough out to a disk, ½ inch thick. Cut out the biscuits with a 2-inch round cutter and re-roll any scraps until you have 16 biscuits. Preheat the air fryer to 164°C. Working in batches, arrange the biscuits in the air fryer basket in a single layer. Bake for about 18 minutes until the biscuits are golden brown. Remove from the basket to a plate and repeat with the remaining biscuits. Serve hot.

Tomato and Cheddar Rolls

Prep time: 30 minutes | Cook time: 25 minutes | Makes 12 rolls

4 plum tomatoes
½ clove garlic, minced
1 tablespoon olive oil
¼ teaspoon dried thyme
Salt and freshly ground black pepper, to taste
1 L plain flour
1 teaspoon active dry yeast

2 teaspoons sugar
2 teaspoons salt
1 tablespoon olive oil
235 ml grated Cheddar cheese, plus more for sprinkling at the end
350 ml water

Cut the tomatoes in half, remove the seeds with your fingers and transfer to a bowl. Add the garlic, olive oil, dried thyme, salt and freshly ground black pepper and toss well. Preheat the air fryer to 200°C. Place the tomatoes, cut side up in the air fryer basket and air fry for 10 minutes. The tomatoes should just start to brown. Shake the basket to redistribute the tomatoes, and air fry for another 5 to 10 minutes at 166°C until the tomatoes are no longer juicy. Let the tomatoes cool and then rough chop them. Combine the flour, yeast, sugar and salt in the bowl of a stand mixer. Add the olive oil, chopped roasted tomatoes and Cheddar cheese to the flour mixture and start to mix using the dough hook attachment.

As you're mixing, add 300 ml of the water, mixing until the dough comes together. Continue to knead the dough with the dough hook for another 10 minutes, adding enough water to the dough to get it to the right consistency. Transfer the dough to an oiled bowl, cover with a clean kitchen towel and let it rest and rise until it has doubled in volume, about 1 to 2 hours. Then, divide the dough into 12 equal portions. Roll each portion of dough into a ball. Lightly coat each dough ball with oil and let the dough balls rest and rise a second time, covered lightly with plastic wrap for 45 minutes. (Alternately, you can place the rolls in the refrigerator overnight and take them out 2 hours before you bake them.) Preheat the air fryer to 182°C. Spray the dough balls and the air fryer basket with a little olive oil. Place three rolls at a time in the basket and bake for 10 minutes. Add a little grated Cheddar cheese on top of the rolls for the last 2 minutes of air frying for an attractive finish.

Cauliflower Avocado Toast

Prep time: 15 minutes | Cook time: 8 minutes | Serves 2

1 (40 g) steamer bag cauliflower
1 large egg
120 ml shredded Mozzarella cheese

1 ripe medium avocado
½ teaspoon garlic powder
¼ teaspoon ground black pepper

Cook cauliflower according to package instructions. Remove from bag and place into cheesecloth or clean towel to remove excess moisture. Place cauliflower into a large bowl and mix in egg and Mozzarella. Cut a piece of parchment to fit your air fryer basket. Separate the cauliflower mixture into two, and place it on the parchment in two mounds. Press out the cauliflower mounds into a ¼-inch-thick rectangle. Place the parchment into the air fryer basket. Adjust the temperature to 204°C and set the timer for 8 minutes. Flip the cauliflower halfway through the cooking time. When the timer beeps, remove the parchment and allow the cauliflower to cool 5 minutes. Cut open the avocado and remove the pit. Scoop out the inside, place it in a medium bowl, and mash it with garlic powder and pepper. Spread onto the cauliflower. Serve immediately.

Cheddar Soufflés

Prep time: 15 minutes | Cook time: 12 minutes | Serves 4

3 large eggs, whites and yolks separated
¼ teaspoon cream of tartar

120 ml shredded sharp Cheddar cheese
85 g cream cheese, softened

In a large bowl, beat egg whites together with cream of tartar until soft peaks form, about 2 minutes. In a separate medium bowl, beat egg yolks, Cheddar, and cream cheese together until frothy, about 1 minute. Add egg yolk mixture to whites, gently folding until combined. Pour mixture evenly into four ramekins greased with cooking spray. Place ramekins into air fryer basket. Adjust the temperature to 176°C and bake for 12 minutes. Eggs will be browned on the top and firm in the center when done. Serve warm.

Smoky Sausage Patties

Prep time: 30 minutes | Cook time: 9 minutes | Serves 8

450 g pork mince
1 tablespoon soy sauce or tamari
1 teaspoon smoked paprika
1 teaspoon dried sage
1 teaspoon sea salt
½ teaspoon fennel seeds
½ teaspoon dried thyme
½ teaspoon freshly ground black pepper
¼ teaspoon cayenne pepper

In a large bowl, combine the pork, soy sauce, smoked paprika, sage, salt, fennel seeds, thyme, black pepper, and cayenne pepper. Work the meat with your hands until the seasonings are fully incorporated. Shape the mixture into 8 equal-size patties. Using your thumb, make a dent in the center of each patty. Place the patties on a plate and cover with plastic wrap. Refrigerate the patties for at least 30 minutes. Working in batches if necessary, place the patties in a single layer in the air fryer, being careful not to overcrowd them. Set the air fryer to 204°C and air fry for 5 minutes. Flip and cook for about 4 minutes more.

Double-Dipped Mini Cinnamon Biscuits

Prep time: 15 minutes | Cook time: 13 minutes | Makes 8 biscuits

475 ml blanched almond flour
120 ml liquid or powdered sweetener
1 teaspoon baking powder
½ teaspoon fine sea salt
60 ml plus 2 tablespoons (¾ stick) very cold unsalted butter
60 ml unsweetened, unflavoured almond milk
1 large egg
1 teaspoon vanilla extract
3 teaspoons ground cinnamon
Glaze:
120 ml powdered sweetener
60 ml double cream or unsweetened, unflavoured almond milk

Preheat the air fryer to 176°C. Line a pie pan that fits into your air fryer with parchment paper. In a medium-sized bowl, mix together the almond flour, sweetener (if powdered; do not add liquid sweetener), baking powder, and salt. Cut the butter into ½-inch squares, then use a hand mixer to work the butter into the dry ingredients. When you are done, the mixture should still have chunks of butter. In a small bowl, whisk together the almond milk, egg, and vanilla extract (if using liquid sweetener, add it as well) until blended. Using a fork, stir the wet ingredients into the dry ingredients until large clumps form. Add the cinnamon and use your hands to swirl it into the dough. Form the dough into sixteen 1-inch balls and place them on the prepared pan, spacing them about ½ inch apart. (If you're using a smaller air fryer, work in batches if necessary.) Bake in the air fryer until golden, 10 to 13 minutes. Remove from the air fryer and let cool on the pan for at least 5 minutes. While the biscuits bake, make the glaze: Place the powdered sweetener in a small bowl and slowly stir in the heavy cream with a fork. When the biscuits have cooled somewhat, dip the tops into the glaze, allow it to dry a bit, and then dip again for a thick glaze. Serve warm or at room temperature. Store unglazed biscuits in an airtight container in the refrigerator for up to 3 days or in the freezer for up to a month. Reheat in a preheated 176°C air fryer for 5 minutes, or until warmed through, and dip in the glaze as instructed above.

Classic British Breakfast

Prep time: 5 minutes | Cook time: 25 minutes | Serves 2

235 ml potatoes, sliced and diced
475 ml baked beans
2 eggs
1 tablespoon olive oil
1 sausage
Salt, to taste

Preheat the air fryer to 200°C and allow to warm. Break the eggs onto a baking dish and sprinkle with salt. Lay the beans on the dish, next to the eggs. In a bowl, coat the potatoes with the olive oil. Sprinkle with salt. Transfer the bowl of potato slices to the air fryer and bake for 10 minutes. Swap out the bowl of potatoes for the dish containing the eggs and beans. Bake for another 10 minutes. Cover the potatoes with parchment paper. Slice up the sausage and throw the slices on top of the beans and eggs. Bake for another 5 minutes. Serve with the potatoes.

Mexican Breakfast Pepper Rings

Prep time: 5 minutes | Cook time: 10 minutes | Serves 4

Olive oil
1 large red, yellow, or orange pepper, cut into four ¾-inch rings
4 eggs
Salt and freshly ground black pepper, to taste
2 teaspoons salsa

Preheat the air fryer to 176°C. Lightly spray a baking pan with olive oil. Place 2 bell pepper rings on the pan. Crack one egg into each bell pepper ring. Season with salt and black pepper. Spoon ½ teaspoon of salsa on top of each egg. Place the pan in the air fryer basket. Air fry until the yolk is slightly runny, 5 to 6 minutes or until the yolk is fully cooked, 8 to 10 minutes. Repeat with the remaining 2 pepper rings. Serve hot.

Three-Berry Dutch Pancake

Prep time: 10 minutes | Cook time: 12 to 16 minutes | Serves 4

2 egg whites
1 egg
120 ml wholemeal plain flour plus 1 tablespoon cornflour
120 ml semi-skimmed milk
1 teaspoon pure vanilla extract
1 tablespoon unsalted butter, melted
235 ml sliced fresh strawberries
120 ml fresh blueberries
120 ml fresh raspberries

In a medium bowl, use an eggbeater or hand mixer to quickly mix the egg whites, egg, flour, milk, and vanilla until well combined. Use a pastry brush to grease the bottom of a baking pan with the melted butter. Immediately pour in the batter and put the basket back in the fryer. Bake at 166°C for 12 to 16 minutes, or until the pancake is puffed and golden brown. Remove the pan from the air fryer; the pancake will fall. Top with the strawberries, blueberries, and raspberries. Serve immediately.

Pitta and Pepperoni Pizza

Prep time: 10 minutes | Cook time: 6 minutes | Serves 1

1 teaspoon olive oil
1 tablespoon pizza sauce
1 pitta bread
6 pepperoni slices
60 ml grated Mozzarella cheese
¼ teaspoon garlic powder
¼ teaspoon dried oregano

Preheat the air fryer to 176°C. Grease the air fryer basket with olive oil. Spread the pizza sauce on top of the pitta bread. Put the pepperoni slices over the sauce, followed by the Mozzarella cheese. Season with garlic powder and oregano. Put the pitta pizza inside the air fryer and place a trivet on top. Bake in the preheated air fryer for 6 minutes and serve.

Baked Peach Oatmeal

Prep time: 5 minutes | Cook time: 30 minutes | Serves 6

Olive oil cooking spray
475 ml certified gluten-free rolled oats
475 ml unsweetened almond milk
60 ml honey, plus more for drizzling (optional)
120 ml non-fat plain Greek yoghurt
1 teaspoon vanilla extract
½ teaspoon ground cinnamon
¼ teaspoon salt
350 ml diced peaches, divided, plus more for serving (optional)

Preheat the air fryer to 192°C. Lightly coat the inside of a 6-inch cake pan with olive oil cooking spray. In a large bowl, mix together the oats, almond milk, honey, yoghurt, vanilla, cinnamon, and salt until well combined. Fold in 180 ml peaches and then pour the mixture into the prepared cake pan. Sprinkle the remaining peaches across the top of the oatmeal mixture. Bake in the air fryer for 30 minutes. Allow to set and cool for 5 minutes before serving with additional fresh fruit and honey for drizzling, if desired.

Maple Granola

Prep time: 5 minutes | Cook time: 40 minutes | Makes 475 ml

235 ml rolled oats
3 tablespoons pure maple syrup
1 tablespoon sugar
1 tablespoon neutral-flavored oil, such as refined coconut or
sunflower
¼ teaspoon sea salt
¼ teaspoon ground cinnamon
¼ teaspoon vanilla extract

Insert the crisper plate into the basket and the basket into the unit. Preheat the unit by selecting BAKE, setting the temperature to 120°C, and setting the time to 3 minutes. Select START/STOP to begin. In a medium bowl, stir together the oats, maple syrup, sugar, oil, salt, cinnamon, and vanilla until thoroughly combined. Transfer the granola to a 6-by-2-inch round baking pan. Once the unit is preheated, place the pan into the basket. Select BAKE, set the temperature to 120°C and set the time to 40 minutes. Select START/STOP to begin. After 10 minutes, stir the granola well. Resume cooking, stirring the granola every 10 minutes, for a total of 40 minutes, or until the granola is lightly browned and mostly dry. When the cooking is complete, place the granola on a plate to cool. It will become crisp as it cools. Store the completely cooled granola in an airtight container in a cool, dry place for 1 to 2 weeks.

Cheddar Eggs

Prep time: 5 minutes | Cook time: 15 minutes | Serves 2

4 large eggs
2 tablespoons unsalted butter, melted
120 ml shredded sharp Cheddar cheese

Crack eggs into a round baking dish and whisk. Place dish into the air fryer basket. Adjust the temperature to 204°C and set the timer for 10 minutes. After 5 minutes, stir the eggs and add the butter and cheese. Let cook 3 more minutes and stir again. Allow eggs to finish cooking an additional 2 minutes or remove if they are to your desired liking. Use a fork to fluff. Serve warm.

Egg Tarts

Prep time: 10 minutes | Cook time: 17 to 20 minutes | Makes 2 tarts

⅓ sheet frozen puff pastry, thawed
Cooking oil spray
120 ml shredded Cheddar cheese
2 eggs
¼ teaspoon salt, divided
1 teaspoon minced fresh parsley (optional)

Insert the crisper plate into the basket and the basket into the unit. Preheat the unit by selecting BAKE, setting the temperature to 200°C, and setting the time to 3 minutes. Select START/STOP to begin. Lay the puff pastry sheet on a piece of parchment paper and cut it in half. Once the unit is preheated, spray the crisper plate with cooking oil. Transfer the 2 squares of pastry to the basket, keeping them on the parchment paper. Select BAKE, set the temperature to 200°C, and set the time to 20 minutes. Select START/STOP to begin. After 10 minutes, use a metal spoon to press down the center of each pastry square to make a well. Divide the cheese equally between the baked pastries. Carefully crack an egg on top of the cheese, and sprinkle each with the salt. Resume cooking for 7 to 10 minutes. When the cooking is complete, the eggs will be cooked through. Sprinkle each with parsley (if using) and serve.

Chapter 2 Vegetarian Mains

Chapter 2 Vegetarian Mains

Sweet Potatoes with Courgette

Prep time: 20 minutes | Cook time: 20 minutes | Serves 4

2 large-sized sweet potatoes, peeled and quartered
1 medium courgette, sliced
1 Serrano or jalapeño pepper, deseeded and thinly sliced
1 pepper, deseeded and thinly sliced
1 to 2 carrots, cut into matchsticks
60 ml olive oil
1½ tablespoons maple syrup
½ teaspoon porcini powder or paste
¼ teaspoon mustard powder
½ teaspoon fennel seeds
1 tablespoon garlic powder
½ teaspoon fine sea salt
¼ teaspoon ground black pepper
Tomato ketchup, for serving

Put the sweet potatoes, courgette, peppers, and the carrot into the air fryer basket. Coat with a drizzling of olive oil. Preheat the air fryer to 176°C. Air fry the vegetables for 15 minutes. In the meantime, prepare the sauce by vigorously combining the other ingredients, except for the tomato ketchup, with a whisk. Lightly grease a baking dish. Transfer the cooked vegetables to the baking dish, pour over the sauce and coat the vegetables well. Increase the temperature to 200°C and air fry the vegetables for an additional 5 minutes. Serve warm with a side of ketchup.

Buffalo Cauliflower Bites with Blue Cheese

Prep time: 10 minutes | Cook time: 8 to 10 minutes | Serves 4

1 large head cauliflower, chopped into florets
1 tablespoon olive oil
Salt and freshly ground black pepper, to taste
60 ml unsalted butter, melted
60 ml hot sauce
Garlic Blue Cheese Dip:
120 ml mayonnaise
60 ml sour cream
2 tablespoons double cream
1 tablespoon fresh lemon juice
1 clove garlic, minced
60 ml crumbled blue cheese
Salt and freshly ground black pepper, to taste

Preheat the air fryer to 204°C. In a large bowl, combine the cauliflower and olive oil. Season to taste with salt and black pepper. Toss until the vegetables are thoroughly coated. Working in batches, place half of the cauliflower in the air fryer basket. Pausing halfway through the cooking time to shake the basket, air fry for 8 to 10 minutes until the cauliflower is evenly browned. Transfer to a large bowl and repeat with the remaining cauliflower. In a small bowl, whisk together the melted butter and hot sauce. To make the dip: In a small bowl, combine the mayonnaise, sour cream, double cream, lemon juice, garlic, and blue cheese. Season to taste with salt and freshly ground black pepper. Just before serving, pour the butter mixture over the cauliflower and toss gently until thoroughly coated. Serve with the dip on the side.

Crispy Tofu

Prep time: 30 minutes | Cook time: 15 to 20 minutes | Serves 4

1 (454 g) block extra-firm tofu
2 tablespoons coconut aminos
1 tablespoon toasted sesame oil
1 tablespoon olive oil
1 tablespoon chilli-garlic sauce
1½ teaspoons black sesame seeds
1 spring onion, thinly sliced

Press the tofu for at least 15 minutes by wrapping it in paper towels and setting a heavy pan on top so that the moisture drains. Slice the tofu into bite-size cubes and transfer to a bowl. Drizzle with the coconut aminos, sesame oil, olive oil, and chilli-garlic sauce. Cover and refrigerate for 1 hour or up to overnight. Preheat the air fryer to 204°C. Arrange the tofu in a single layer in the air fryer basket. Pausing to shake the pan halfway through the cooking time, air fry for 15 to 20 minutes until crisp. Serve with any juices that accumulate in the bottom of the air fryer, sprinkled with the sesame seeds and sliced spring onion.

Garlic White Courgette Rolls

Prep time: 20 minutes | Cook time: 20 minutes | Serves 4

2 medium courgette
2 tablespoons unsalted butter
¼ white onion, peeled and diced
½ teaspoon finely minced roasted garlic
60 ml double cream
2 tablespoons vegetable broth
⅛ teaspoon xanthan gum
120 ml full-fat ricotta cheese
¼ teaspoon salt
½ teaspoon garlic powder
¼ teaspoon dried oregano
475 ml spinach, chopped
120 ml sliced baby portobello mushrooms
180 ml shredded Mozzarella cheese, divided

Using a mandoline or sharp knife, slice courgette into long strips lengthwise. Place strips between paper towels to absorb moisture. Set aside. In a medium saucepan over medium heat, melt butter. Add onion and sauté until fragrant. Add garlic and sauté 30 seconds. Pour in double cream, broth, and xanthan gum. Turn off heat and whisk mixture until it begins to thicken, about 3 minutes. In a medium bowl, add ricotta, salt, garlic powder, and oregano and mix well. Fold in spinach, mushrooms, and 120 ml Mozzarella. Pour half of the sauce into a round baking pan. To assemble the rolls, place two strips of courgette on a work surface. Spoon 2 tablespoons of ricotta mixture onto the slices and roll up. Place seam side down on top of sauce. Repeat with remaining ingredients. Pour remaining sauce over the rolls and sprinkle with remaining Mozzarella. Cover with foil and place into the air fryer basket. Adjust the temperature to 176°C and bake for 20 minutes. In the last 5 minutes, remove the foil to brown the cheese. Serve immediately.

Pesto Vegetable Skewers

Prep time: 30 minutes | Cook time: 8 minutes | Makes 8 skewers

1 medium courgette, trimmed and cut into ½-inch slices
½ medium brown onion, peeled and cut into 1-inch squares
1 medium red pepper, seeded and cut into 1-inch squares

16 whole cremini or chestnut mushrooms
80 ml basil pesto
½ teaspoon salt
¼ teaspoon ground black pepper

Divide courgette slices, onion, and pepper into eight even portions. Place on 6-inch skewers for a total of eight kebabs. Add 2 mushrooms to each skewer and brush kebabs generously with pesto. Sprinkle each kebab with salt and black pepper on all sides, then place into ungreased air fryer basket. Adjust the temperature to 192°C and air fry for 8 minutes, turning kebabs halfway through cooking. Vegetables will be browned at the edges and tender-crisp when done. Serve warm.

Sweet Pepper Nachos

Prep time: 10 minutes | Cook time: 5 minutes | Serves 2

6 mini sweet peppers, seeded and sliced in half
180 ml shredded Colby jack or Monterey Jack cheese

60 ml sliced pickled jalapeños
½ medium avocado, peeled, pitted, and diced
2 tablespoons sour cream

Place peppers into an ungreased round non-stick baking dish. Sprinkle with cheese and top with jalapeños. Place dish into air fryer basket. Adjust the temperature to 176°C and bake for 5 minutes. Cheese will be melted and bubbly when done. Remove dish from air fryer and top with avocado. Drizzle with sour cream. Serve warm.

Aubergine Parmesan

Prep time: 15 minutes | Cook time: 17 minutes | Serves 4

1 medium aubergine, ends trimmed, sliced into ½-inch rounds
¼ teaspoon salt
2 tablespoons coconut oil
120 ml grated Parmesan cheese

30 g cheese crisps, finely crushed
120 ml low-carb marinara sauce
120 ml shredded Mozzarella cheese

Sprinkle aubergine rounds with salt on both sides and wrap in a kitchen towel for 30 minutes. Press to remove excess water, then drizzle rounds with coconut oil on both sides. In a medium bowl, mix Parmesan and cheese crisps. Press each aubergine slice into mixture to coat both sides. Place rounds into ungreased air fryer basket. Adjust the temperature to 176°C and air fry for 15 minutes, turning rounds halfway through cooking. They will be crispy around the edges when done. Spoon marinara over rounds and sprinkle with Mozzarella. Continue cooking an additional 2 minutes at 176°C until cheese is melted. Serve warm.

Lush Summer Rolls

Prep time: 15 minutes | Cook time: 15 minutes | Serves 4

235 ml shiitake mushroom, sliced thinly
1 celery stalk, chopped
1 medium carrot, shredded
½ teaspoon finely chopped ginger

1 teaspoon sugar
1 tablespoon soy sauce
1 teaspoon Engevita yeast flakes
8 spring roll sheets
1 teaspoon corn starch
2 tablespoons water

In a bowl, combine the ginger, soy sauce, Engevita yeast flakes, carrots, celery, mushroom, and sugar. Mix the cornflour and water to create an adhesive for the spring rolls. Scoop a tablespoonful of the vegetable mixture into the middle of the spring roll sheets. Brush the edges of the sheets with the cornflour adhesive and enclose around the filling to make spring rolls. Preheat the air fryer to 204°C. When warm, place the rolls inside and air fry for 15 minutes or until crisp. Serve hot.

Potato and Broccoli with Tofu Scramble

Prep time: 15 minutes | Cook time: 30 minutes | Serves 3

600 ml chopped red potato
2 tablespoons olive oil, divided
1 block tofu, chopped finely
2 tablespoons tamari
1 teaspoon turmeric powder

½ teaspoon onion powder
½ teaspoon garlic powder
120 ml chopped onion
1 L broccoli florets

Preheat the air fryer to 204°C. Toss together the potatoes and 1 tablespoon of the olive oil. Air fry the potatoes in a baking dish for 15 minutes, shaking once during the cooking time to ensure they fry evenly. Combine the tofu, the remaining 1 tablespoon of the olive oil, turmeric, onion powder, tamari, and garlic powder together, stirring in the onions, followed by the broccoli. Top the potatoes with the tofu mixture and air fry for an additional 15 minutes. Serve warm.

Cheese Stuffed Peppers

Prep time: 20 minutes | Cook time: 15 minutes | Serves 2

1 red pepper, top and seeds removed
1 yellow pepper, top and seeds removed

Salt and pepper, to taste
235 ml Cottage cheese
4 tablespoons mayonnaise
2 pickles, chopped

Arrange the peppers in the lightly greased air fryer basket. Cook in the preheated air fryer at 204°C for 15 minutes, turning them over halfway through the cooking time. Season with salt and pepper. Then, in a mixing bowl, combine the soft white cheese with the mayonnaise and chopped pickles. Stuff the pepper with the soft white cheese mixture and serve. Enjoy!

Cauliflower Steak with Gremolata

Prep time: 15 minutes | Cook time: 25 minutes | Serves 4

2 tablespoons olive oil
1 tablespoon Italian seasoning
1 large head cauliflower, outer leaves removed and sliced lengthwise through the core into thick "steaks"
Salt and freshly ground black pepper, to taste

60 ml Parmesan cheese
Gremolata:
1 bunch Italian parsley
2 cloves garlic
Zest of 1 small lemon, plus 1 to 2 teaspoons lemon juice
120 ml olive oil
Salt and pepper, to taste

Preheat the air fryer to 204°C. In a small bowl, combine the olive oil and Italian seasoning. Brush both sides of each cauliflower "steak" generously with the oil. Season to taste with salt and black pepper. Working in batches if necessary, arrange the cauliflower in a single layer in the air fryer basket. Pausing halfway through the cooking time to turn the "steaks," air fry for 15 to 20 minutes until the cauliflower is tender and the edges begin to brown. Sprinkle with the Parmesan and air fry for 5 minutes longer. To make the gremolata: In a food processor fitted with a metal blade, combine the parsley, garlic, and lemon zest and juice. With the motor running, add the olive oil in a steady stream until the mixture forms a bright green sauce. Season to taste with salt and black pepper. Serve the cauliflower steaks with the gremolata spooned over the top.

Baked Turnip and Courgette

Prep time: 5 minutes | Cook time: 15 to 20 minutes | Serves 4

3 turnips, sliced
1 large courgette, sliced
1 large red onion, cut into rings

2 cloves garlic, crushed
1 tablespoon olive oil
Salt and black pepper, to taste

Preheat the air fryer to 166°C. Put the turnips, courgette, red onion, and garlic in a baking pan. Drizzle the olive oil over the top and sprinkle with the salt and pepper. Place the baking pan in the preheated air fryer and bake for 15 to 20 minutes, or until the vegetables are tender. Remove from the basket and serve on a plate.

Crustless Spinach Cheese Pie

Prep time: 10 minutes | Cook time: 20 minutes | Serves 4

6 large eggs
60 ml double cream
235 ml frozen chopped spinach, drained

235 ml shredded sharp Cheddar cheese
60 ml diced brown onion

In a medium bowl, whisk eggs and add cream. Add remaining ingredients to bowl. Pour into a round baking dish. Place into the air fryer basket. Adjust the temperature to 160°C and bake for 20 minutes. Eggs will be firm and slightly browned when cooked. Serve immediately.

Crispy Cabbage Steaks

Prep time: 5 minutes | Cook time: 10 minutes | Serves 4

1 small head green cabbage, cored and cut into ½-inch-thick slices
¼ teaspoon salt
¼ teaspoon ground black pepper

2 tablespoons olive oil
1 clove garlic, peeled and finely minced
½ teaspoon dried thyme
½ teaspoon dried parsley

Sprinkle each side of cabbage with salt and pepper, then place into ungreased air fryer basket, working in batches if needed. Drizzle each side of cabbage with olive oil, then sprinkle with remaining ingredients on both sides. Adjust the temperature to 176°C and air fry for 10 minutes, turning "steaks" halfway through cooking. 3.Cabbage will be browned at the edges and tender when done. Serve warm.

Air Fryer Winter Vegetables

Prep time: 5 minutes | Cook time: 16 minutes | Serves 2

1 parsnip, sliced
235 ml sliced butternut squash
1 small red onion, cut into wedges
½ chopped celery stalk

1 tablespoon chopped fresh thyme
2 teaspoons olive oil
Salt and black pepper, to taste

Preheat the air fryer to 192°C. Toss all the ingredients in a large bowl until the vegetables are well coated. Transfer the vegetables to the air fryer basket and air fry for 16 minutes, shaking the basket halfway through, or until the vegetables are golden brown and tender. Remove from the basket and serve warm.

Fried Root Vegetable Medley with Thyme

Prep time: 10 minutes | Cook time: 22 minutes | Serves 4

2 carrots, sliced
2 potatoes, cut into chunks
1 swede, cut into chunks
1 turnip, cut into chunks
1 beetroot, cut into chunks
8 shallots, halved

2 tablespoons olive oil
Salt and black pepper, to taste
2 tablespoons tomato pesto
2 tablespoons water
2 tablespoons chopped fresh thyme

Preheat the air fryer to 204°C. Toss the carrots, potatoes, swede, turnip, beetroot, shallots, olive oil, salt, and pepper in a large mixing bowl until the root vegetables are evenly coated. Place the root vegetables in the air fryer basket and air fry for 12 minutes. Shake the basket and air fry for another 10 minutes until they are cooked to your preferred doneness. Meanwhile, in a small bowl, whisk together the tomato pesto and water until smooth. When ready, remove the root vegetables from the basket to a platter. Drizzle with the tomato pesto mixture and sprinkle with the thyme. Serve immediately.

Air Fryer Veggies with Halloumi

Prep time: 5 minutes | Cook time: 14 minutes | Serves 2

2 courgettes, cut into even chunks
1 large aubergine, peeled, cut into chunks
1 large carrot, cut into chunks
170 g halloumi cheese, cubed
2 teaspoons olive oil
Salt and black pepper, to taste
1 teaspoon dried mixed herbs

Preheat the air fryer to 172°C. Combine the courgettes, aubergine, carrot, cheese, olive oil, salt, and pepper in a large bowl and toss to coat well. Spread the mixture evenly in the air fryer basket and air fry for 14 minutes until crispy and golden, shaking the basket once during cooking. Serve topped with mixed herbs.

Cheesy Cauliflower Pizza Crust

Prep time: 15 minutes | Cook time: 11 minutes | Serves 2

1 (340 g) steamer bag cauliflower
120 ml shredded extra mature Cheddar cheese
1 large egg
2 tablespoons blanched finely ground almond flour
1 teaspoon Italian blend seasoning

Cook cauliflower according to package instructions. Remove from bag and place into cheesecloth or paper towel to remove excess water. Place cauliflower into a large bowl. Add cheese, egg, almond flour, and Italian seasoning to the bowl and mix well. Cut a piece of parchment to fit your air fryer basket. Press cauliflower into 6-inch round circle. Place into the air fryer basket. Adjust the temperature to 182°C and air fry for 11 minutes. After 7 minutes, flip the pizza crust. Add preferred toppings to pizza. Place back into air fryer basket and cook an additional 4 minutes or until fully cooked and golden. Serve immediately.

Spaghetti Squash Alfredo

Prep time: 10 minutes | Cook time: 15 minutes | Serves 2

½ large cooked spaghetti squash
2 tablespoons salted butter, melted
120 ml low-carb Alfredo sauce
60 ml grated vegetarian Parmesan cheese
½ teaspoon garlic powder
1 teaspoon dried parsley
¼ teaspoon ground peppercorn
120 ml shredded Italian blend cheese

Using a fork, remove the strands of spaghetti squash from the shell. Place into a large bowl with butter and Alfredo sauce. Sprinkle with Parmesan, garlic powder, parsley, and peppercorn. Pour into a 1 L round baking dish and top with shredded cheese. Place dish into the air fryer basket. Adjust the temperature to 160°C and bake for 15 minutes. When finished, cheese will be golden and bubbling. Serve immediately.

Broccoli with Garlic Sauce

Prep time: 19 minutes | Cook time: 15 minutes | Serves 4

2 tablespoons olive oil
Rock salt and freshly ground black pepper, to taste
450 g broccoli florets
Dipping Sauce:
2 teaspoons dried rosemary,
crushed
3 garlic cloves, minced
⅓ teaspoon dried marjoram, crushed
60 ml sour cream
80 ml mayonnaise

Lightly grease your broccoli with a thin layer of olive oil. Season with salt and ground black pepper. Arrange the seasoned broccoli in the air fryer basket. Bake at 202°C for 15 minutes, shaking once or twice. In the meantime, prepare the dipping sauce by mixing all the sauce ingredients. Serve warm broccoli with the dipping sauce and enjoy!

Stuffed Portobellos

Prep time: 10 minutes | Cook time: 8 minutes | Serves 4

85 g soft white cheese
½ medium courgette, trimmed and chopped
60 ml seeded and chopped red pepper
350 ml chopped fresh spinach
leaves
4 large portobello mushrooms, stems removed
2 tablespoons coconut oil, melted
½ teaspoon salt

In a medium bowl, mix soft white cheese, courgette, pepper, and spinach. Drizzle mushrooms with coconut oil and sprinkle with salt. Scoop ¼ courgette mixture into each mushroom. Place mushrooms into ungreased air fryer basket. Adjust the temperature to 204°C and air fry for 8 minutes. Portobellos will be tender, and tops will be browned when done. Serve warm.

Teriyaki Cauliflower

Prep time: 5 minutes | Cook time: 14 minutes | Serves 4

120 ml soy sauce
80 ml water
1 tablespoon brown sugar
1 teaspoon sesame oil
1 teaspoon cornflour
2 cloves garlic, chopped
½ teaspoon chilli powder
1 big cauliflower head, cut into florets

Preheat the air fryer to 172°C. Make the teriyaki sauce: In a small bowl, whisk together the soy sauce, water, brown sugar, sesame oil, cornflour, garlic, and chilli powder until well combined. Place the cauliflower florets in a large bowl and drizzle the top with the prepared teriyaki sauce and toss to coat well. Put the cauliflower florets in the air fryer basket and air fry for 14 minutes, shaking the basket halfway through, or until the cauliflower is crisp-tender. Let the cauliflower cool for 5 minutes before serving.

Baked Courgette

Prep time: 10 minutes | Cook time: 8 minutes | Serves 4

2 tablespoons salted butter	60 g full fat soft white cheese
60 ml diced white onion	235 ml shredded extra mature
½ teaspoon minced garlic	Cheddar cheese
120 ml double cream	2 medium courgette, spiralized

In a large saucepan over medium heat, melt butter. Add onion and sauté until it begins to soften, 1 to 3 minutes. Add garlic and sauté for 30 seconds, then pour in cream and add soft white cheese. Remove the pan from heat and stir in Cheddar. Add the courgette and toss in the sauce, then put into a round baking dish. Cover the dish with foil and place into the air fryer basket. Adjust the temperature to 188ºC and set the timer for 8 minutes. After 6 minutes remove the foil and let the top brown for remaining cooking time. Stir and serve.

Caprese Aubergine Stacks

Prep time: 5 minutes | Cook time: 12 minutes | Serves 4

1 medium aubergine, cut into ¼-inch slices	110 g fresh Mozzarella, cut into 14 g slices
2 large tomatoes, cut into ¼-inch slices	2 tablespoons olive oil
	60 ml fresh basil, sliced

In a baking dish, place four slices of aubergine on the bottom. Place a slice of tomato on top of each aubergine round, then Mozzarella, then aubergine. Repeat as necessary. Drizzle with olive oil. Cover dish with foil and place dish into the air fryer basket. Adjust the temperature to 176ºC and bake for 12 minutes. When done, aubergine will be tender. Garnish with fresh basil to serve.

Cheesy Cabbage Wedges

Prep time: 5 minutes | Cook time: 20 minutes | Serves 4

4 tablespoons melted butter	Salt and black pepper, to taste
1 head cabbage, cut into wedges	120 ml shredded Mozzarella cheese
235 ml shredded Parmesan cheese	

Preheat the air fryer to 192ºC. Brush the melted butter over the cut sides of cabbage wedges and sprinkle both sides with the Parmesan cheese. Season with salt and pepper to taste. Place the cabbage wedges in the air fryer basket and air fry for 20 minutes, flipping the cabbage halfway through, or until the cabbage wedges are lightly browned. Transfer the cabbage wedges to a plate and serve with the Mozzarella cheese sprinkled on top.

Quiche-Stuffed Peppers

Prep time: 5 minutes | Cook time: 15 minutes | Serves 2

2 medium green peppers	120 ml chopped broccoli
3 large eggs	120 ml shredded medium
60 ml full-fat ricotta cheese	Cheddar cheese
60 ml diced brown onion	

Cut the tops off of the peppers and remove the seeds and white membranes with a small knife. In a medium bowl, whisk eggs and ricotta. Add onion and broccoli. Pour the egg and vegetable mixture evenly into each pepper. Top with Cheddar. Place peppers into a 1 L round baking dish and place into the air fryer basket. Adjust the temperature to 176ºC and bake for 15 minutes. Eggs will be mostly firm and peppers tender when fully cooked. Serve immediately.

Basmati Risotto

Prep time: 10 minutes | Cook time: 30 minutes | Serves 2

1 onion, diced	1 clove garlic, minced
1 small carrot, diced	180 ml long-grain basmati rice
475 ml vegetable broth, boiling	1 tablespoon olive oil
120 ml grated Cheddar cheese	1 tablespoon unsalted butter

Preheat the air fryer to 200ºC. Grease a baking tin with oil and stir in the butter, garlic, carrot, and onion. Put the tin in the air fryer and bake for 4 minutes. Pour in the rice and bake for a further 4 minutes, stirring three times throughout the baking time. Turn the temperature down to 160ºC. Add the vegetable broth and give the dish a gentle stir. Bake for 22 minutes, leaving the air fryer uncovered. Pour in the cheese, stir once more and serve.

Cauliflower, Chickpea, and Avocado Mash

Prep time: 10 minutes | Cook time: 25 minutes | Serves 4

1 medium head cauliflower, cut into florets	2 tablespoons lemon juice
1 can chickpeas, drained and rinsed	Salt and ground black pepper, to taste
1 tablespoon extra-virgin olive oil	4 flatbreads, toasted
	2 ripe avocados, mashed

Preheat the air fryer to 218ºC. In a bowl, mix the chickpeas, cauliflower, lemon juice and olive oil. Sprinkle salt and pepper as desired. Put inside the air fryer basket and air fry for 25 minutes. Spread on top of the flatbread along with the mashed avocado. Sprinkle with more pepper and salt and serve.

Courgette and Spinach Croquettes

4 eggs, slightly beaten
120 ml almond flour
120 ml goat cheese, crumbled
1 teaspoon fine sea salt
4 garlic cloves, minced

235 ml baby spinach
120 ml Parmesan cheese, grated
⅓ teaspoon red pepper flakes
450 g courgette, peeled and grated
⅓ teaspoon dried dill weed

Thoroughly combine all ingredients in a bowl. Now, roll the mixture to form small croquettes. Air fry at 172°C for 7 minutes or until golden. Tate, adjust for seasonings and serve warm.

Broccoli Crust Pizza

700 ml riced broccoli, steamed and drained well
1 large egg
120 ml grated vegetarian Parmesan cheese

3 tablespoons low-carb Alfredo sauce
120 ml shredded Mozzarella cheese

In a large bowl, mix broccoli, egg, and Parmesan. Cut a piece of parchment to fit your air fryer basket. Press out the pizza mixture to fit on the parchment, working in two batches if necessary. Place into the air fryer basket. Adjust the temperature to 188°C and air fry for 5 minutes. The crust should be firm enough to flip. If not, add 2 additional minutes. Flip crust. Top with Alfredo sauce and Mozzarella. Return to the air fryer basket and cook an additional 7 minutes or until cheese is golden and bubbling. Serve warm.

Chapter 3 Poultry

Chapter 3 Poultry

Crisp Paprika Chicken Drumsticks

Prep time: 5 minutes | Cook time: 22 minutes | Serves 2

2 teaspoons paprika
1 teaspoon packed brown sugar
1 teaspoon garlic powder
½ teaspoon dry mustard
½ teaspoon salt
Pinch pepper

4 (140 g) chicken drumsticks, trimmed
1 teaspoon vegetable oil
1 scallion, green part only, sliced thin on bias

Preheat the air fryer to 200°C. Combine paprika, sugar, garlic powder, mustard, salt, and pepper in a bowl. Pat drumsticks dry with paper towels. Using metal skewer, poke 10 to 15 holes in skin of each drumstick. Rub with oil and sprinkle evenly with spice mixture. Arrange drumsticks in air fryer basket, spaced evenly apart, alternating ends. Air fry until chicken is crisp and registers 90°C, 22 to 25 minutes, flipping chicken halfway through cooking. Transfer chicken to serving platter, tent loosely with aluminum foil, and let rest for 5 minutes. Sprinkle with scallion and serve.

Coriander Lime Chicken Thighs

Prep time: 15 minutes | Cook time: 22 minutes | Serves 4

4 bone-in, skin-on chicken thighs
1 teaspoon baking powder
½ teaspoon garlic powder

2 teaspoons chili powder
1 teaspoon cumin
2 medium limes
5 g chopped fresh coriander

Pat chicken thighs dry and sprinkle with baking powder. In a small bowl, mix garlic powder, chili powder, and cumin and sprinkle evenly over thighs, gently rubbing on and under chicken skin. Cut one lime in half and squeeze juice over thighs. Place chicken into the air fryer basket. Adjust the temperature to 190°C and roast for 22 minutes. Cut other lime into four wedges for serving and garnish cooked chicken with wedges and coriander.

Barbecued Chicken with Creamy Coleslaw

Prep time: 10 minutes | Cook time: 20 minutes | Serves 2

270 g shredded coleslaw mix
Salt and pepper
2 (340 g) bone-in split chicken breasts, trimmed
1 teaspoon vegetable oil
2 tablespoons barbecue sauce,

plus extra for serving
2 tablespoons mayonnaise
2 tablespoons sour cream
1 teaspoon distilled white vinegar, plus extra for seasoning
¼ teaspoon sugar

Preheat the air fryer to 180°C. Toss coleslaw mix and ¼ teaspoon salt in a colander set over bowl. Let sit until wilted slightly, about 30 minutes. Rinse, drain, and dry well with a dish towel. Meanwhile, pat chicken dry with paper towels, rub with oil, and season with salt and pepper. Arrange breasts skin-side down in air fryer basket, spaced evenly apart, alternating ends. Bake for 10 minutes. Flip breasts and brush skin side with barbecue sauce. Return basket to air fryer and bake until well browned and chicken registers 70°C, 10 to 15 minutes. Transfer chicken to serving platter, tent loosely with aluminum foil, and let rest for 5 minutes. While chicken rests, whisk mayonnaise, sour cream, vinegar, sugar, and pinch pepper together in a large bowl. Stir in coleslaw mix and season with salt, pepper, and additional vinegar to taste. Serve chicken with coleslaw, passing extra barbecue sauce separately.

Chicken Shawarma

Prep time: 30 minutes | Cook time: 15 minutes | Serves 4

Shawarma Spice:
2 teaspoons dried oregano
1 teaspoon ground cinnamon
1 teaspoon ground cumin
1 teaspoon ground coriander
1 teaspoon kosher salt
½ teaspoon ground allspice
½ teaspoon cayenne pepper

Chicken:
450 g boneless, skinless chicken thighs, cut into large bite-size chunks
2 tablespoons vegetable oil
For Serving:
Tzatziki
Pita bread

For the shawarma spice: In a small bowl, combine the oregano, cayenne, cumin, coriander, salt, cinnamon, and allspice. For the chicken: In a large bowl, toss together the chicken, vegetable oil, and shawarma spice to coat. Marinate at room temperature for 30 minutes or cover and refrigerate for up to 24 hours. Place the chicken in the air fryer basket. Set the air fryer to 180°C for 15 minutes, or until the chicken reaches an internal temperature of 76°C. Transfer the chicken to a serving platter. Serve with tzatziki and pita bread.

Italian Chicken Thighs

Prep time: 5 minutes | Cook time: 20 minutes | Serves 2

4 bone-in, skin-on chicken thighs
2 tablespoons unsalted butter, melted
1 teaspoon dried parsley

1 teaspoon dried basil
½ teaspoon garlic powder
¼ teaspoon onion powder
¼ teaspoon dried oregano

Brush chicken thighs with butter and sprinkle remaining ingredients over thighs. Place thighs into the air fryer basket. Adjust the temperature to 190°C and roast for 20 minutes. Halfway through the cooking time, flip the thighs. When fully cooked, internal temperature will be at least 76°C and skin will be crispy. Serve warm.

Cranberry Curry Chicken

Prep time: 12 minutes | Cook time: 18 minutes | Serves 4

3 (140 g) low-sodium boneless, skinless chicken breasts, cut into 1½-inch cubes
2 teaspoons olive oil
2 tablespoons cornflour
1 tablespoon curry powder
1 tart apple, chopped

120 ml low-sodium chicken broth
60 g dried cranberries
2 tablespoons freshly squeezed orange juice
Brown rice, cooked (optional)

Preheat the air fryer to 196ºC. In a medium bowl, mix the chicken and olive oil. Sprinkle with the cornflour and curry powder. Toss to coat. Stir in the apple and transfer to a metal pan. Bake in the air fryer for 8 minutes, stirring once during cooking. Add the chicken broth, cranberries, and orange juice. Bake for about 10 minutes more, or until the sauce is slightly thickened and the chicken reaches an internal temperature of 76ºC on a meat thermometer. Serve over hot cooked brown rice, if desired.

Spice-Rubbed Turkey Breast

Prep time: 5 minutes | Cook time: 45 to 55 minutes | Serves 10

1 tablespoon sea salt
1 teaspoon paprika
1 teaspoon onion powder
1 teaspoon garlic powder
½ teaspoon freshly ground black

pepper
1.8 kg bone-in, skin-on turkey breast
2 tablespoons unsalted butter, melted

In a small bowl, combine the salt, paprika, onion powder, garlic powder, and pepper. Sprinkle the seasonings all over the turkey. Brush the turkey with some of the melted butter. Set the air fryer to 180ºC. . Place the turkey in the air fryer basket, skin-side down, and roast for 25 minutes. Flip the turkey and brush it with the remaining butter. Continue cooking for another 20 to 30 minutes, until an instant-read thermometer reads 70ºC. Remove the turkey breast from the air fryer. Tent a piece of aluminum foil over the turkey, and allow it to rest for about 5 minutes before serving.

Garlic Parmesan Drumsticks

Prep time: 5 minutes | Cook time: 25 minutes | Serves 4

8 (115 g) chicken drumsticks
½ teaspoon salt
⅛ teaspoon ground black pepper
½ teaspoon garlic powder

2 tablespoons salted butter, melted
45 g grated Parmesan cheese
1 tablespoon dried parsley

Sprinkle drumsticks with salt, pepper, and garlic powder. Place drumsticks into ungreased air fryer basket. Adjust the temperature to 200ºC and air fry for 25 minutes, turning drumsticks halfway through cooking. Drumsticks will be golden and have an internal temperature of at least 76ºC when done. Transfer drumsticks to a large serving dish. Pour butter over drumsticks, and sprinkle with Parmesan and parsley. Serve warm.

Coconut Chicken Wings with Mango Sauce

Prep time: 15 minutes | Cook time: 20 minutes | Serves 4

16 chicken drumettes (party wings)
60 ml full-fat coconut milk
1 tablespoon sriracha
1 teaspoon onion powder
1 teaspoon garlic powder
Salt and freshly ground black pepper, to taste
25 g shredded unsweetened

coconut
60 g all-purpose flour
Cooking oil spray
165 g mango, cut into ½-inch chunks
15 g fresh coriander, chopped
25 g red onion, chopped
2 garlic cloves, minced
Juice of ½ lime

Place the drumettes in a resealable plastic bag. In a small bowl, whisk the coconut milk and sriracha. Drizzle the drumettes with the sriracha–coconut milk mixture. Season the drumettes with the onion powder, garlic powder, salt, and pepper. Seal the bag. Shake it thoroughly to combine the seasonings and coat the chicken. Marinate for at least 30 minutes, preferably overnight, in the refrigerator. When the drumettes are almost done marinating, in a large bowl, stir together the shredded coconut and flour. Dip the drumettes into the coconut-flour mixture. Press the flour mixture onto the chicken with your hands. Insert the crisper plate into the basket and the basket into the unit. Preheat the unit by selecting AIR FRY, setting the temperature to 200ºC, and setting the time to 3 minutes. Select START/STOP to begin. Once the unit is preheated, spray the crisper plate and the basket with cooking oil. Place the drumettes in the air fryer. It is okay to stack them. Spray the drumettes with cooking oil, being sure to cover the bottom layer. Select AIR FRY, set the temperature to 200ºC, and set the time to 20 minutes. Select START/STOP to begin. After 5 minutes, remove the basket and shake it to ensure all pieces cook through. Reinsert the basket to resume cooking. Remove and shake the basket every 5 minutes, twice more, until a food thermometer inserted into the drumettes registers 76ºC. 1When the cooking is complete, let the chicken cool for 5 minutes. 1While the chicken cooks and cools, make the salsa. In a small bowl, combine the mango, coriander, red onion, garlic, and lime juice. Mix well until fully combined. Serve with the wings.

Blackened Chicken

Prep time: 10 minutes | Cook time: 20 minutes | Serves 4

1 large egg, beaten
215 g Blackened seasoning
2 whole boneless, skinless

chicken breasts (about 450 g each), halved
1 to 2 tablespoons oil

Place the beaten egg in one shallow bowl and the Blackened seasoning in another shallow bowl. One at a time, dip the chicken pieces in the beaten egg and the Blackened seasoning, coating thoroughly. Preheat the air fryer to 180ºC. Line the air fryer basket with parchment paper. Place the chicken pieces on the parchment and spritz with oil. Cook for 10 minutes. Flip the chicken, spritz it with oil, and cook for 10 minutes more until the internal temperature reaches 76ºC and the chicken is no longer pink inside. Let sit for 5 minutes before serving.

Nice Goulash

Prep time: 5 minutes | Cook time: 17 minutes | Serves 2

2 red bell peppers, chopped
450 g chicken mince
2 medium tomatoes, diced
120 ml chicken broth
Salt and ground black pepper, to taste
Cooking spray

Preheat the air fryer to 186°C. Spritz a baking pan with cooking spray. Set the bell pepper in the baking pan and put in the air fry to broil for 5 minutes or until the bell pepper is tender. Shake the basket halfway through. Add the chicken mince and diced tomatoes in the baking pan and stir to mix well. Broil for 6 more minutes or until the chicken is lightly browned. Pour the chicken broth over and sprinkle with salt and ground black pepper. Stir to mix well. Broil for an additional 6 minutes. Serve immediately.

Bacon-Wrapped Stuffed Chicken Breasts

Prep time: 15 minutes | Cook time: 30 minutes | Serves 4

80 g chopped frozen spinach, thawed and squeezed dry
55 g cream cheese, softened
20 g grated Parmesan cheese
1 jalapeño, seeded and chopped
½ teaspoon kosher salt
1 teaspoon black pepper
2 large boneless, skinless chicken breasts, butterflied and pounded to ½-inch thickness
4 teaspoons salt-free Cajun seasoning
6 slices bacon

In a small bowl, combine the spinach, cream cheese, Parmesan cheese, jalapeño, salt, and pepper. Stir until well combined. Place the butterflied chicken breasts on a flat surface. Spread the cream cheese mixture evenly across each piece of chicken. Starting with the narrow end, roll up each chicken breast, ensuring the filling stays inside. Season chicken with the Cajun seasoning, patting it in to ensure it sticks to the meat. Wrap each breast in 3 slices of bacon. Place in the air fryer basket. Set the air fryer to 180°C for 30 minutes. Use a meat thermometer to ensure the chicken has reached an internal temperature of 76°C. Let the chicken stand 5 minutes before slicing each rolled-up breast in half to serve.

Buttermilk Breaded Chicken

Prep time: 7 minutes | Cook time: 20 to 25 minutes | Serves 4

125 g all-purpose flour
2 teaspoons paprika
Pinch salt
Freshly ground black pepper, to taste
80 ml buttermilk
2 eggs
2 tablespoons extra-virgin olive oil
185 g bread crumbs
6 chicken pieces, drumsticks, breasts, and thighs, patted dry
Cooking oil spray

In a shallow bowl, stir together the flour, paprika, salt, and pepper. In another bowl, beat the buttermilk and eggs until smooth. In a third bowl, stir together the olive oil and bread crumbs until mixed.

Dredge the chicken in the flour, dip in the eggs to coat, and finally press into the bread crumbs, patting the crumbs firmly onto the chicken skin. Insert the crisper plate into the basket and the basket into the unit. Preheat the unit by selecting AIR FRY, setting the temperature to 190°C, and setting the time to 3 minutes. Select START/STOP to begin. Once the unit is preheated, spray the crisper plate with cooking oil. Place the chicken into the basket. Select AIR FRY, set the temperature to 190°C, and set the time to 25 minutes. Select START/STOP to begin. After 10 minutes, flip the chicken. Resume cooking. After 10 minutes more, check the chicken. If a food thermometer inserted into the chicken registers 76°C and the chicken is brown and crisp, it is done. Otherwise, resume cooking for up to 5 minutes longer. When the cooking is complete, let cool for 5 minutes, then serve.

Simply Terrific Turkey Meatballs

Prep time: 10 minutes | Cook time: 7 to 10 minutes | Serves 4

1 red bell pepper, seeded and coarsely chopped
2 cloves garlic, coarsely chopped
15 g chopped fresh parsley
680 g 85% lean turkey mince
1 egg, lightly beaten
45 g grated Parmesan cheese
1 teaspoon salt
½ teaspoon freshly ground black pepper

Preheat the air fryer to 200°C. In a food processor fitted with a metal blade, combine the bell pepper, garlic, and parsley. Pulse until finely chopped. Transfer the vegetables to a large mixing bowl. Add the turkey, egg, Parmesan, salt, and black pepper. Mix gently until thoroughly combined. Shape the mixture into 1¼-inch meatballs. Working in batches if necessary, arrange the meatballs in a single layer in the air fryer basket; coat lightly with olive oil spray. Pausing halfway through the cooking time to shake the basket, air fry for 7 to 10 minutes, until lightly browned and a thermometer inserted into the centre of a meatball registers 76°C.

Classic Whole Chicken

Prep time: 5 minutes | Cook time: 50 minutes | Serves 4

Oil, for spraying
1 (1.8 kg) whole chicken, giblets removed
1 tablespoon olive oil
1 teaspoon paprika
½ teaspoon granulated garlic
½ teaspoon salt
½ teaspoon freshly ground black pepper
¼ teaspoon finely chopped fresh parsley, for garnish

Line the air fryer basket with parchment and spray lightly with oil. Pat the chicken dry with paper towels. Rub it with the olive oil until evenly coated. In a small bowl, mix together the paprika, garlic, salt, and black pepper and sprinkle it evenly over the chicken. Place the chicken in the prepared basket, breast-side down. Air fry at 180°C for 30 minutes, flip, and cook for another 20 minutes, or until the internal temperature reaches 76°C and the juices run clear. Sprinkle with the parsley before serving.

Cheese-Encrusted Chicken Tenderloins with Peanuts

Prep time: 10 minutes | Cook time: 25 minutes | Serves 4

45 g grated Parmesan cheese
½ teaspoon garlic powder
1 teaspoon red pepper flakes
Sea salt and ground black pepper, to taste

2 tablespoons peanut oil
680 g chicken tenderloins
2 tablespoons peanuts, roasted and roughly chopped
Cooking spray

Preheat the air fryer to 180°C. Spritz the air fryer basket with cooking spray. Combine the Parmesan cheese, garlic powder, red pepper flakes, salt, black pepper, and peanut oil in a large bowl. Stir to mix well. Dip the chicken tenderloins in the cheese mixture, then press to coat well. Shake the excess off. Transfer the chicken tenderloins in the air fryer basket. Air fry for 12 minutes or until well browned. Flip the tenderloin halfway through. You may need to work in batches to avoid overcrowding. Transfer the chicken tenderloins on a large plate and top with roasted peanuts before serving.

Cracked-Pepper Chicken Wings

Prep time: 15 minutes | Cook time: 20 minutes | Serves 4

450 g chicken wings
3 tablespoons vegetable oil
60 g all-purpose flour
½ teaspoon smoked paprika

½ teaspoon garlic powder
½ teaspoon kosher salt
1½ teaspoons freshly cracked black pepper

Place the chicken wings in a large bowl. Drizzle the vegetable oil over wings and toss to coat. In a separate bowl, whisk together the flour, paprika, garlic powder, salt, and pepper until combined. Dredge the wings in the flour mixture one at a time, coating them well, and place in the air fryer basket. Set the air fryer to 200°C for 20 minutes, turning the wings halfway through the cooking time, until the breading is browned and crunchy.

Herbed Roast Chicken Breast

Prep time: 10 minutes | Cook time: 25 minutes | Serves 2 to 4

2 tablespoons salted butter or ghee, at room temperature
1 teaspoon dried Italian seasoning, crushed
½ teaspoon kosher salt

½ teaspoon smoked paprika
¼ teaspoon black pepper
2 bone-in, skin-on chicken breast halves (280 g each)
Lemon wedges, for serving

In a small bowl, stir together the butter, Italian seasoning, salt, paprika, and pepper until thoroughly combined. Using a small sharp knife, carefully loosen the skin on each chicken breast half, starting at the thin end of each. Very carefully separate the skin from the flesh, leaving the skin attached at the thick end of each breast. Divide the herb butter into quarters. Rub one-quarter of the butter onto the flesh of each breast. Fold and lightly press the skin back onto each breast. Rub the remaining butter onto the skin of each breast. Place the chicken in the air fryer basket. Set the air fryer to (190°C for 25 minutes. Use a meat thermometer to ensure the chicken breasts have reached an internal temperature of 76°C. Transfer the chicken to a cutting board. Lightly cover with aluminum foil and let rest for 5 to 10 minutes. Serve with lemon wedges.

Stuffed Turkey Roulade

Prep time: 10 minutes | Cook time: 45 minutes | Serves 4

1 (900 g) boneless turkey breast, skin removed
1 teaspoon salt
½ teaspoon black pepper
115 g goat cheese
1 tablespoon fresh thyme

1 tablespoon fresh sage
2 garlic cloves, minced
2 tablespoons olive oil
Fresh chopped parsley, for garnish

Preheat the air fryer to 192°C. Using a sharp knife, butterfly the turkey breast, and season both sides with salt and pepper and set aside. In a small bowl, mix together the goat cheese, thyme, sage, and garlic. Spread the cheese mixture over the turkey breast, then roll it up tightly, tucking the ends underneath. Place the turkey breast roulade onto a piece of aluminum foil, wrap it up, and place it into the air fryer. Bake for 30 minutes. Remove the foil from the turkey breast and brush the top with oil, then continue cooking for another 10 to 15 minutes, or until the outside has browned and the internal temperature reaches 76°C. Remove and cut into 1-inch-wide slices and serve with a sprinkle of parsley on top.

Greek Chicken Souvlaki

Prep time: 30 minutes | Cook time: 15 minutes | Serves 3 to 4

Chicken:
Grated zest and juice of 1 lemon
2 tablespoons extra-virgin olive oil
1 tablespoon Greek souvlaki seasoning
450 g boneless, skinless chicken breast, cut into 2-inch chunks
Vegetable oil spray

For Serving:
Warm pita bread or hot cooked rice
Sliced ripe tomatoes
Sliced cucumbers
Thinly sliced red onion
Kalamata olives
Tzatziki

For the chicken: In a small bowl, combine the lemon zest, lemon juice, olive oil, and souvlaki seasoning. Place the chicken in a gallon-size resealable plastic bag. Pour the marinade over chicken. Seal bag and massage to coat. Place the bag in a large bowl and marinate for 30 minutes, or cover and refrigerate up to 24 hours, turning the bag occasionally. Place the chicken a single layer in the air fryer basket. Set the air fryer to 180°C for 10 minutes, turning the chicken and spraying with a little vegetable oil spray halfway through the cooking time. Increase the air fryer temperature to 200°C for 5 minutes to allow the chicken to crisp and brown a little. Transfer the chicken to a serving platter and serve with pita bread or rice, tomatoes, cucumbers, onion, olives and tzatziki.

Lemon Thyme Roasted Chicken

Prep time: 10 minutes | Cook time: 60 minutes | Serves 6

2 tablespoons baking powder	80 ml avocado oil
1 teaspoon smoked paprika	120 ml Buffalo hot sauce, such
Sea salt and freshly ground	as Frank's RedHot
black pepper, to taste	4 tablespoons unsalted butter
900 g chicken wings or chicken	2 tablespoons apple cider
drumettes	vinegar
Avocado oil spray	1 teaspoon minced garlic

In a large bowl, stir together the baking powder, smoked paprika, and salt and pepper to taste. Add the chicken wings and toss to coat. Set the air fryer to 200°C. Spray the wings with oil. Place the wings in the basket in a single layer, working in batches, and air fry for 20 to 25 minutes. Check with an instant-read thermometer and remove when they reach 70°C. Let rest until they reach 76°C. While the wings are cooking, whisk together the avocado oil, hot sauce, butter, vinegar, and garlic in a small saucepan over medium-low heat until warm. When the wings are done cooking, toss them with the Buffalo sauce. Serve warm.

Fajita-Stuffed Chicken Breast

Prep time: 15 minutes | Cook time: 25 minutes | Serves 4

2 (170 g) boneless, skinless	seeded and sliced
chicken breasts	1 tablespoon coconut oil
¼ medium white onion, peeled	2 teaspoons chili powder
and sliced	1 teaspoon ground cumin
1 medium green bell pepper,	½ teaspoon garlic powder

Slice each chicken breast completely in half lengthwise into two even pieces. Using a meat tenderizer, pound out the chicken until it's about ¼-inch thickness. Lay each slice of chicken out and place three slices of onion and four slices of green pepper on the end closest to you. Begin rolling the peppers and onions tightly into the chicken. Secure the roll with either toothpicks or a couple pieces of butcher's twine. Drizzle coconut oil over chicken. Sprinkle each side with chili powder, cumin, and garlic powder. Place each roll into the air fryer basket. Adjust the temperature to 180°C and air fry for 25 minutes. Serve warm.

Jalapeño Popper Hasselback Chicken

Prep time: 10 minutes | Cook time: 19 minutes | Serves 2

Oil, for spraying	55 g bacon bits
2 (230 g) boneless, skinless	20 g chopped pickled jalapeños
chicken breasts	40 g shredded Cheddar cheese,
60 g cream cheese, softened	divided

Line the air fryer basket with parchment and spray lightly with oil. Make multiple cuts across the top of each chicken breast, cutting only halfway through. In a medium bowl, mix together the cream cheese, bacon bits, jalapeños, and Cheddar cheese. Spoon some of the mixture into each cut. Place the chicken in the prepared basket. Air fry at 176°C for 14 minutes. Scatter the remaining cheese on top of the chicken and cook for another 2 to 5 minutes, or until the cheese is melted and the internal temperature reaches 76°C.

Chicken and Gruyère Cordon Bleu

Prep time: 15 minutes | Cook time: 15 minutes | Serves 4

4 chicken breast filets	Freshly ground black pepper, to
75 g chopped ham	taste
75 g grated Swiss cheese, or	½ teaspoon dried marjoram
Gruyère cheese	1 egg
30 g all-purpose flour	120 g panko bread crumbs
Pinch salt	Olive oil spray

Put the chicken breast filets on a work surface and gently press them with the palm of your hand to make them a bit thinner. Don't tear the meat. In a small bowl, combine the ham and cheese. Divide this mixture among the chicken filets. Wrap the chicken around the filling to enclose it, using toothpicks to hold the chicken together. In a shallow bowl, stir together the flour, salt, pepper, and marjoram. In another bowl, beat the egg. Spread the panko on a plate. Dip the chicken in the flour mixture, in the egg, and in the panko to coat thoroughly. Press the crumbs into the chicken so they stick well. Insert the crisper plate into the basket and the basket into the unit. Preheat the unit by selecting BAKE, setting the temperature to 190°C, and setting the time to 3 minutes. Select START/STOP to begin. Once the unit is preheated, spray the crisper plate with olive oil. Place the chicken into the basket and spray it with olive oil. Select BAKE, set the temperature to 190°C, and set the time to 15 minutes. Select START/STOP to begin. 1When the cooking is complete, the chicken should be cooked through and a food thermometer inserted into the chicken should register 76°C. Carefully remove the toothpicks and serve.

Spanish Chicken and Mini Sweet Pepper Baguette

Prep time: 10 minutes | Cook time: 20 minutes | Serves 2

570 g assorted small chicken	60 g light mayonnaise
parts, breasts cut into halves	¼ teaspoon smoked paprika
¼ teaspoon salt	½ clove garlic, crushed
¼ teaspoon ground black pepper	Baguette, for serving
2 teaspoons olive oil	Cooking spray
230 g mini sweet peppers	

Preheat air fryer to 190°C. Spritz the air fryer basket with cooking spray. Toss the chicken with salt, ground black pepper, and olive oil in a large bowl. Arrange the sweet peppers and chicken in the preheated air fryer and air fry for 10 minutes, then transfer the peppers on a plate. Flip the chicken and air fry for 10 more minutes or until well browned. Meanwhile, combine the mayo, paprika, and garlic in a small bowl. Stir to mix well. Assemble the baguette with chicken and sweet pepper, then spread with mayo mixture and serve.

Gochujang Chicken Wings

Prep time: 15 minutes | Cook time: 25 minutes | Serves 4

Wings:
900 g chicken wings
1 teaspoon kosher salt
1 teaspoon black pepper or
gochugaru (Korean red pepper)
Sauce:
2 tablespoons gochujang
(Korean chili paste)
1 tablespoon mayonnaise
1 tablespoon toasted sesame oil

1 tablespoon minced fresh
ginger
1 tablespoon minced garlic
1 teaspoon sugar
1 teaspoon agave nectar or
honey
For Serving
1 teaspoon sesame seeds
25 g chopped spring onions

For the wings: Season the wings with the salt and pepper and place in the air fryer basket. Set the air fryer to 200ºC for 20 minutes, turning the wings halfway through the cooking time. Meanwhile, for the sauce: In a small bowl, combine the gochujang, mayonnaise, sesame oil, ginger, garlic, sugar, and agave; set aside. As you near the 20-minute mark, use a meat thermometer to check the meat. When the wings reach 70ºC, transfer them to a large bowl. Pour about half the sauce on the wings; toss to coat (serve the remaining sauce as a dip). Return the wings to the air fryer basket and cook for 5 minutes, until the sauce has glazed. Transfer the wings to a serving platter. Sprinkle with the sesame seeds and spring onions. Serve with the reserved sauce on the side for dipping.

Chicken Breasts with Asparagus, Beans, and Rocket

Prep time: 20 minutes | Cook time: 25 minutes | Serves 2

160 g canned cannellini beans,
rinsed
1½ tablespoons red wine
vinegar
1 garlic clove, minced
2 tablespoons extra-virgin olive
oil, divided
Salt and ground black pepper, to
taste

½ red onion, sliced thinly
230 g asparagus, trimmed and
cut into 1-inch lengths
2 (230 g) boneless, skinless
chicken breasts, trimmed
¼ teaspoon paprika
½ teaspoon ground coriander
60 g baby rocket, rinsed and
drained

Preheat the air fryer to 200ºC. Warm the beans in microwave for 1 minutes and combine with red wine vinegar, garlic, 1 tablespoon of olive oil, ¼ teaspoon of salt, and ¼ teaspoon of ground black pepper in a bowl. Stir to mix well. Combine the onion with ⅛ teaspoon of salt, ⅛ teaspoon of ground black pepper, and 2 teaspoons of olive oil in a separate bowl. Toss to coat well. Place the onion in the air fryer and air fry for 2 minutes, then add the asparagus and air fry for 8 more minutes or until the asparagus is tender. Shake the basket halfway through. Transfer the onion and asparagus to the bowl with beans. Set aside. Toss the chicken breasts with remaining ingredients, except for the baby rocket, in a large bowl. Put the chicken breasts in the air fryer and air fry for 14 minutes or until the internal temperature of the chicken reaches at least 76ºC. Flip the breasts halfway through. Remove the chicken from the air fryer and serve on an aluminum foil with asparagus, beans, onion, and rocket. Sprinkle with salt and ground black pepper. Toss to serve.

Chicken Drumsticks with Barbecue-Honey Sauce

Prep time: 5 minutes | Cook time: 40 minutes | Serves 5

1 tablespoon olive oil
10 chicken drumsticks
Chicken seasoning or rub, to
taste

Salt and ground black pepper, to
taste
240 ml barbecue sauce
85 g honey

Preheat the air fryer to 200ºC. Grease the air fryer basket with olive oil. Rub the chicken drumsticks with chicken seasoning or rub, salt and ground black pepper on a clean work surface. Arrange the chicken drumsticks in a single layer in the air fryer, then air fry for 18 minutes or until lightly browned. Flip the drumsticks halfway through. You may need to work in batches to avoid overcrowding. Meanwhile, combine the barbecue sauce and honey in a small bowl. Stir to mix well. Remove the drumsticks from the air fryer and baste with the sauce mixture to serve.

Apricot-Glazed Chicken Drumsticks

Prep time: 15 minutes | Cook time: 30 minutes | Makes 6 drumsticks

For the Glaze:
160 g apricot preserves
½ teaspoon tamari
¼ teaspoon chili powder
2 teaspoons Dijon mustard
For the Chicken:

6 chicken drumsticks
½ teaspoon seasoning salt
1 teaspoon salt
½ teaspoon ground black pepper
Cooking spray

Make the glaze: Combine the ingredients for the glaze in a saucepan, then heat over low heat for 10 minutes or until thickened. Turn off the heat and sit until ready to use. Make the Chicken: Preheat the air fryer to 190ºC. Spritz the air fryer basket with cooking spray. Combine the seasoning salt, salt, and pepper in a small bowl. Stir to mix well. Place the chicken drumsticks in the preheated air fryer. Spritz with cooking spray and sprinkle with the salt mixture on both sides. Air fry for 20 minutes or until well browned. Flip the chicken halfway through. Baste the chicken with the glaze and air fryer for 2 more minutes or until the chicken tenderloin is glossy. Serve immediately.

Buffalo Chicken Cheese Sticks

Prep time: 5 minutes | Cook time: 8 minutes | Serves 2

140 g shredded cooked chicken
60 ml buffalo sauce
220 g shredded Mozzarella

cheese
1 large egg
55 g crumbled feta

In a large bowl, mix all ingredients except the feta. Cut a piece of parchment to fit your air fryer basket and press the mixture into a ½-inch-thick circle. Sprinkle the mixture with feta and place into the air fryer basket. Adjust the temperature to 200ºC and air fry for 8 minutes. After 5 minutes, flip over the cheese mixture. Allow to cool 5 minutes before cutting into sticks. Serve warm.

Quick Chicken Fajitas

Prep time: 10 minutes | Cook time: 15 minutes | Serves 2

280 g boneless, skinless chicken breast, sliced into ¼-inch strips
2 tablespoons coconut oil, melted
1 tablespoon chili powder
½ teaspoon cumin
½ teaspoon paprika
½ teaspoon garlic powder
¼ medium onion, peeled and sliced
½ medium green bell pepper, seeded and sliced
½ medium red bell pepper, seeded and sliced

Place chicken and coconut oil into a large bowl and sprinkle with chili powder, cumin, paprika, and garlic powder. Toss chicken until well coated with seasoning. Place chicken into the air fryer basket. Adjust the temperature to 180°C and air fry for 15 minutes. Add onion and peppers into the basket when the cooking time has 7 minutes remaining. Toss the chicken two or three times during cooking. Vegetables should be tender and chicken fully cooked to at least 76°C internal temperature when finished. Serve warm.
adas on each plate and top with more enchilada sauce, if desired.

Potato-Crusted Chicken

Prep time: 15 minutes | Cook time: 22 to 25 minutes | Serves 4

60 g buttermilk
1 large egg, beaten
180 g instant potato flakes
20 g grated Parmesan cheese
1 teaspoon salt
½ teaspoon freshly ground black
pepper
2 whole boneless, skinless chicken breasts (about 450 g each), halved
1 to 2 tablespoons oil

In a shallow bowl, whisk the buttermilk and egg until blended. In another shallow bowl, stir together the potato flakes, cheese, salt, and pepper. One at a time, dip the chicken pieces in the buttermilk mixture and the potato flake mixture, coating thoroughly. Preheat the air fryer to 200°C. Line the air fryer basket with parchment paper. Place the coated chicken on the parchment and spritz with oil. Cook for 15 minutes. Flip the chicken, spritz it with oil, and cook for 7 to 10 minutes more until the outside is crispy and the inside is no longer pink.

Mediterranean Stuffed Chicken Breasts

Prep time: 5 minutes | Cook time: 20 to 25 minutes | Serves 4

4 small boneless, skinless chicken breast halves (about 680 g)
Salt and freshly ground black pepper, to taste
115 g goat cheese
6 pitted Kalamata olives, coarsely chopped
Zest of ½ lemon
1 teaspoon minced fresh rosemary or ½ teaspoon ground dried rosemary
50 g almond meal
60 ml balsamic vinegar
6 tablespoons unsalted butter

Preheat the air fryer to 180°C. With a boning knife, cut a wide pocket into the thickest part of each chicken breast half, taking care not to cut all the way through. Season the chicken evenly on both sides with salt and freshly ground black pepper. In a small bowl, mix the cheese, olives, lemon zest, and rosemary. Stuff the pockets with the cheese mixture and secure with toothpicks. Place the almond meal in a shallow bowl and dredge the chicken, shaking off the excess. Coat lightly with olive oil spray. Working in batches if necessary, arrange the chicken breasts in a single layer in the air fryer basket. Pausing halfway through the cooking time to flip the chicken, air fry for 20 to 25 minutes, until a thermometer inserted into the thickest part registers 76°C. While the chicken is baking, prepare the sauce. In a small pan over medium heat, simmer the balsamic vinegar until thick and syrupy, about 5 minutes. Set aside until the chicken is done. When ready to serve, warm the sauce over medium heat and whisk in the butter, 1 tablespoon at a time, until melted and smooth. Season to taste with salt and pepper. Serve the chicken breasts with the sauce drizzled on top.

Lemon-Dijon Boneless Chicken

Prep time: 30 minutes | Cook time: 13 to 16 minutes | Serves 6

115 g sugar-free mayonnaise
1 tablespoon Dijon mustard
1 tablespoon freshly squeezed lemon juice (optional)
1 tablespoon coconut aminos
1 teaspoon Italian seasoning
1 teaspoon sea salt
½ teaspoon freshly ground black pepper
¼ teaspoon cayenne pepper
680 g boneless, skinless chicken breasts or thighs

In a small bowl, combine the mayonnaise, mustard, lemon juice (if using), coconut aminos, Italian seasoning, salt, black pepper, and cayenne pepper. Place the chicken in a shallow dish or large zip-top plastic bag. Add the marinade, making sure all the pieces are coated. Cover and refrigerate for at least 30 minutes or up to 4 hours. Set the air fryer to 200°C. Arrange the chicken in a single layer in the air fryer basket, working in batches if necessary. Air fry for 7 minutes. Flip the chicken and continue cooking for 6 to 9 minutes more, until an instant-read thermometer reads 70°C.

Golden Chicken Cutlets

Prep time: 15 minutes | Cook time: 15 minutes | Serves 4

2 tablespoons panko breadcrumbs
20 g grated Parmesan cheese
⅛ tablespoon paprika
½ tablespoon garlic powder
2 large eggs
4 chicken cutlets
1 tablespoon parsley
Salt and ground black pepper, to taste
Cooking spray

Preheat air fryer to 200°C. Spritz the air fryer basket with cooking spray. Combine the breadcrumbs, Parmesan, paprika, garlic powder, salt, and ground black pepper in a large bowl. Stir to mix well. Beat the eggs in a separate bowl. Dredge the chicken cutlets in the beaten eggs, then roll over the breadcrumbs mixture to coat well. Shake the excess off. Transfer the chicken cutlets in the preheated air fryer and spritz with cooking spray. Air fry for 15 minutes or until crispy and golden brown. Flip the cutlets halfway through. Serve with parsley on top.

Breaded Turkey Cutlets

Prep time: 5 minutes | Cook time: 8 minutes | Serves 4

60 g whole wheat bread crumbs	⅛ teaspoon garlic powder
¼ teaspoon paprika	1 egg
¼ teaspoon salt	4 turkey breast cutlets
¼ teaspoon black pepper	Chopped fresh parsley, for
⅛ teaspoon dried sage	serving

Preheat the air fryer to 192°C. In a medium shallow bowl, whisk together the bread crumbs, paprika, salt, black pepper, sage, and garlic powder. In a separate medium shallow bowl, whisk the egg until frothy. Dip each turkey cutlet into the egg mixture, then into the bread crumb mixture, coating the outside with the crumbs. Place the breaded turkey cutlets in a single layer in the bottom of the air fryer basket, making sure that they don't touch each other. Bake for 4 minutes. Turn the cutlets over, then bake for 4 minutes more, or until the internal temperature reaches 76°C. Sprinkle on the parsley and serve.

Crunchy Chicken Tenders

Prep time: 5 minutes | Cook time: 12 minutes | Serves 4

1 egg	½ teaspoon dried thyme
60 ml unsweetened almond milk	½ teaspoon dried sage
30 g whole wheat flour	½ teaspoon garlic powder
30 g whole wheat bread crumbs	450 g chicken tenderloins
½ teaspoon salt	1 lemon, quartered
½ teaspoon black pepper	

Preheat the air fryer to 184°C. In a shallow bowl, beat together the egg and almond milk until frothy. In a separate shallow bowl, whisk together the flour, bread crumbs, salt, pepper, thyme, sage, and garlic powder. Dip each chicken tenderloin into the egg mixture, then into the bread crumb mixture, coating the outside with the crumbs. Place the breaded chicken tenderloins into the bottom of the air fryer basket in an even layer, making sure that they don't touch each other. Cook for 6 minutes, then turn and cook for an additional 5 to 6 minutes. Serve with lemon slices.

Smoky Chicken Leg Quarters

Prep time: 30 minutes | Cook time: 23 to 27 minutes | Serves 6

120 ml avocado oil	½ teaspoon dried thyme
2 teaspoons smoked paprika	½ teaspoon freshly ground black
1 teaspoon sea salt	pepper
1 teaspoon garlic powder	900 g bone-in, skin-on chicken
½ teaspoon dried rosemary	leg quarters

In a blender or small bowl, combine the avocado oil, smoked paprika, salt, garlic powder, rosemary, thyme, and black pepper. Place the chicken in a shallow dish or large zip-top bag. Pour the marinade over the chicken, making sure all the legs are coated. Cover and marinate for at least 2 hours or overnight. Place the chicken in a single layer in the air fryer basket, working in batches if necessary. Set the air fryer to 200°C and air fry for 15 minutes. Flip the chicken legs, then reduce the temperature to 180°C. . Cook for 8 to 12 minutes more, until an instant-read thermometer reads 70°C when inserted into the thickest piece of chicken. Allow to rest for 5 to 10 minutes before serving.

Ethiopian Chicken with Cauliflower

Prep time: 15 minutes | Cook time: 28 minutes | Serves 6

2 handful fresh Italian parsley, roughly chopped	⅓ teaspoon porcini powder
20 g fresh chopped chives	1½ teaspoons berbere spice
2 sprigs thyme	⅓ teaspoon sweet paprika
6 chicken drumsticks	½ teaspoon shallot powder
1½ small-sized head cauliflower, broken into large-sized florets	1teaspoon granulated garlic
2 teaspoons mustard powder	1 teaspoon freshly cracked pink peppercorns
	½ teaspoon sea salt

Simply combine all items for the berbere spice rub mix. After that, coat the chicken drumsticks with this rub mix on all sides. Transfer them to the baking dish. Now, lower the cauliflower onto the chicken drumsticks. Add thyme, chives and Italian parsley and spritz everything with a pan spray. Transfer the baking dish to the preheated air fryer. Next step, set the timer for 28 minutes; roast at 180°C, turning occasionally. Bon appétit!

Chicken Enchiladas

Prep time: 10 minutes | Cook time: 8 minutes | Serves 4

Oil, for spraying	and drained
420 g shredded cooked chicken	1 (115 g) can diced green
1 package taco seasoning	chilies, drained
8 flour tortillas, at room	1 (280 g) can red or green
temperature	enchilada sauce
60 g canned black beans, rinsed	235 g shredded Cheddar cheese

Line the air fryer basket with parchment and spray lightly with oil. (Do not skip the step of lining the basket; the parchment will keep the sauce and cheese from dripping through the holes.) In a small bowl, mix together the chicken and taco seasoning. Divide the mixture among the tortillas. Top with the black beans and green chilis. Carefully roll up each tortilla. Place the enchiladas, seam-side down, in the prepared basket. You may need to work in batches, depending on the size of your air fryer. Spoon the enchilada sauce over the enchiladas. Use just enough sauce to keep them from drying out. You can add more sauce when serving. Sprinkle the cheese on top. Air fry at 180°C for 5 to 8 minutes, or until heated through and the cheese is melted. Place 2 enchil

Chapter 4 Fish and Seafood

Chapter 4 Fish and Seafood

Sea Bass with Potato Scales

Prep time: 10 minutes | Cook time: 10 minutes | Serves 2

2 fillets of sea bass, 170- to 230 g each	very thinly sliced into rounds
Salt and freshly ground black pepper, to taste	Olive oil
60 ml mayonnaise	½ clove garlic, crushed into a paste
2 teaspoons finely chopped lemon zest	1 tablespoon capers, drained and rinsed
1 teaspoon chopped fresh thyme	1 tablespoon olive oil
2 Fingerling, or new potatoes,	1 teaspoon lemon juice, to taste

Preheat the air fryer to 204ºC. Season the fish well with salt and freshly ground black pepper. Mix the mayonnaise, lemon zest and thyme together in a small bowl. Spread a thin layer of the mayonnaise mixture on both fillets. Start layering rows of potato slices onto the fish fillets to simulate the fish scales. The second row should overlap the first row slightly. Dabbing a little more mayonnaise along the upper edge of the row of potatoes where the next row overlaps will help the potato slices stick. Press the potatoes onto the fish to secure them well and season again with salt. Brush or spray the potato layer with olive oil. Transfer the fish to the air fryer and air fry for 8 to 10 minutes, depending on the thickness of your fillets. 1-inch of fish should take 10 minutes at 204ºC. While the fish is cooking, add the garlic, capers, olive oil and lemon juice to the remaining mayonnaise mixture to make the caper aïoli. Serve the fish warm with a dollop of the aïoli on top or on the side.

Coconut Prawns with Spicy Dipping Sauce

Prep time: 15 minutes | Cook time: 8 minutes | Serves 4

70 g pork scratchings	½ teaspoon salt
70 g desiccated, unsweetened coconut	¼ teaspoon freshly ground black pepper
85 g coconut flour	Spicy Dipping Sauce:
1 teaspoon onion powder	115 g mayonnaise
1 teaspoon garlic powder	2 tablespoons Sriracha
2 eggs	Zest and juice of ½ lime
680 g large prawns, peeled and deveined	1 clove garlic, minced

Preheat the air fryer to 200ºC. In a food processor fitted with a metal blade, combine the pork scratchings and desiccated coconut. Pulse until the mixture resembles coarse crumbs. Transfer to a shallow bowl. In another shallow bowl, combine the coconut flour, onion powder, and garlic powder; mix until thoroughly combined. In a third shallow bowl, whisk the eggs until slightly frothy. In a large bowl, season the prawns with the salt and pepper, tossing gently to coat. Working a few pieces at a time, dredge the prawns in the flour mixture, followed by the eggs, and finishing with the pork rind crumb mixture. Arrange the prawns on a baking sheet until ready to air fry. Working in batches if necessary, arrange the prawns in a single layer in the air fryer basket. Pausing halfway through the cooking time to turn the prawns, air fry for 8 minutes until cooked through. To make the sauce: In a small bowl, combine the mayonnaise, Sriracha, lime zest and juice, and garlic. Whisk until thoroughly combined. Serve alongside the prawns.

Crispy Prawns with Coriander

Prep time: 40 minutes | Cook time: 10 minutes | Serves 4

455 g raw large prawns, peeled and deveined with tails on or off	75 g bread crumbs
30 g chopped fresh coriander	Salt and freshly ground black pepper, to taste
Juice of 1 lime	Cooking oil spray
70 g plain flour	240 ml seafood sauce
1 egg	

Place the prawns in a resealable plastic bag and add the cilantro and lime juice. Seal the bag. Shake it to combine. Marinate the prawns in the refrigerator for 30 minutes. Place the flour in a small bowl. In another small bowl, beat the egg. Place the bread crumbs in a third small bowl, season with salt and pepper, and stir to combine. Insert the crisper plate into the basket and the basket into the unit. Preheat the unit to 204ºC.Remove the prawns from the plastic bag. Dip each in the flour, the egg, and the bread crumbs to coat. Gently press the crumbs onto the prawns. Once the unit is preheated, spray the crisper plate and the basket with cooking oil. Place the prawns in the basket. It is okay to stack them. Spray the prawns with the cooking oil. Cook for 4 minutes, remove the basket and flip the prawns one at a time. Reinsert the basket to resume cooking. 1When the cooking is complete, the prawns should be crisp. Let cool for 5 minutes. Serve with cocktail sauce.

chilli Tilapia

Prep time: 5 minutes | Cook time: 20 minutes | Serves 4

4 tilapia fillets, boneless	1 tablespoon avocado oil
1 teaspoon chilli flakes	1 teaspoon mustard
1 teaspoon dried oregano	

Rub the tilapia fillets with chilli flakes, dried oregano, avocado oil, and mustard and put in the air fryer. Cook it for 10 minutes per side at 182ºC.

Salmon Croquettes

1 tablespoon vegetable oil
75 g breadcrumbs
420 g can salmon, drained and all skin and fat removed
1 egg, beaten
25 g coarsely crushed salted

crackers
½ teaspoon Old Bay Seasoning
½ teaspoon onion powder
½ teaspoon Worcestershire sauce

Preheat the air fryer to 200ºC. In a shallow dish, mix oil and breadcrumbs until crumbly. In a large bowl, combine the salmon, egg, cracker crumbs, Old Bay, onion powder, and Worcestershire. Mix well and shape into 8 small patties about ½-inch thick. Gently dip each patty into bread crumb mixture and turn to coat well on all sides. Cook for 7 to 8 minutes or until outside is crispy and browned.

Catfish Bites

Olive or vegetable oil, for spraying
455 g catfish fillets, cut into 2-inch pieces
235 ml buttermilk

70 g cornmeal
30 g plain flour
2 teaspoons Creole seasoning
120 ml yellow mustard

Line the air fryer basket with baking paper and spray lightly with oil. Place the catfish pieces and buttermilk in a zip-top plastic bag, seal, and refrigerate for about 10 minutes. In a shallow bowl, mix together the cornmeal, flour, and Creole seasoning. Remove the catfish from the bag and pat dry with a paper towel. Spread the mustard on all sides of the catfish, then dip them in the cornmeal mixture until evenly coated. Place the catfish in the prepared basket. You may need to work in batches, depending on the size of your air fryer. Spray lightly with oil. Air fry at 204ºC for 10 minutes, flip carefully, spray with oil, and cook for another 10 minutes. Serve immediately.

Tex-Mex Salmon Bowl

340 g salmon fillets, cut into 1½-inch cubes
1 red onion, chopped
1 jalapeño pepper, minced
1 red bell pepper, chopped

60 ml salsa
2 teaspoons peanut or safflower oil
2 tablespoons tomato juice
1 teaspoon chilli powder

Preheat the air fryer to 188ºC. Mix together the salmon cubes, red onion, jalapeño, red bell pepper, salsa, peanut oil, tomato juice, chilli powder in a medium metal bowl and stir until well incorporated. Transfer the bowl to the air fryer basket and bake for 9 to 14 minutes, stirring once, or until the salmon is cooked through and the veggies are fork-tender. Serve warm.

Salmon Burgers with Creamy Broccoli Slaw

For the salmon burgers
455 g salmon fillets, bones and skin removed
1 egg
10 g fresh dill, chopped
60 g fresh whole wheat bread crumbs
½ teaspoon salt
½ teaspoon cayenne pepper
2 garlic cloves, minced
4 whole wheat buns

For the broccoli slaw
270 g chopped or shredded broccoli
25 g shredded carrots
30 g sunflower seeds
2 garlic cloves, minced
½ teaspoon salt
2 tablespoons apple cider vinegar
285 g nonfat plain Greek yogurt

Make the salmon burgers Preheat the air fryer to 182ºC. In a food processor, pulse the salmon fillets until they are finely chopped. In a large bowl, combine the chopped salmon, egg, dill, bread crumbs, salt, cayenne, and garlic until it comes together. Form the salmon into 4 patties. Place them into the air fryer basket, making sure that they don't touch each other. Bake for 5 minutes. Flip the salmon patties and bake for 5 minutes more. Make the broccoli slaw In a large bowl, combine all of the ingredients for the broccoli slaw. Mix well. Serve the salmon burgers on toasted whole wheat buns, and top with a generous portion of broccoli slaw.

Sole and Asparagus Bundles

230 g asparagus, trimmed
1 teaspoon extra-virgin olive oil, divided
Salt and pepper, to taste
4 (85 g) skinless sole fillets, ⅛ to ¼ inch thick
4 tablespoons unsalted butter,

softened
1 small shallot, minced
1 tablespoon chopped fresh tarragon
¼ teaspoon lemon zest plus ½ teaspoon juice
Vegetable oil spray

Preheat the air fryer to 150ºC. Toss asparagus with ½ teaspoon oil, pinch salt, and pinch pepper in a bowl. Cover and microwave until bright green and just tender, about 3 minutes, tossing halfway through microwaving. Uncover and set aside to cool slightly. Make foil sling for air fryer basket by folding 1 long sheet of aluminum foil so it is 4 inches wide. Lay sheet of foil widthwise across basket, pressing foil into and up sides of basket. Fold excess foil as needed so that edges of foil are flush with top of basket. Lightly spray foil and basket with vegetable oil spray. Pat sole dry with paper towels and season with salt and pepper. Arrange fillets skinned side up on cutting board, with thicker ends closest to you. Arrange asparagus evenly across base of each fillet, then tightly roll fillets away from you around asparagus to form tidy bundles. Rub bundles evenly with remaining ½ teaspoon oil and arrange seam side down on sling in prepared basket. Bake until asparagus is tender and sole flakes apart when gently prodded with a paring knife, 14 to 18 minutes, using a sling to rotate bundles halfway through cooking. Combine butter, shallot, tarragon, and lemon zest and juice in a bowl. Using sling, carefully remove sole bundles from air fryer and transfer to individual plates. Top evenly with butter mixture and serve.

Almond Pesto Salmon

Prep time: 5 minutes | Cook time: 12 minutes | Serves 2

60 g pesto
20 g sliced almonds, roughly chopped
2 (1½-inch-thick) salmon fillets
(about 110 g each)
2 tablespoons unsalted butter, melted

In a small bowl, mix pesto and almonds. Set aside. Place fillets into a round baking dish. Brush each fillet with butter and place half of the pesto mixture on the top of each fillet. Place dish into the air fryer basket. Adjust the temperature to 200°C and set the timer for 12 minutes. Salmon will easily flake when fully cooked and reach an internal temperature of at least 64°C. Serve warm.

Snapper with Shallot and Tomato

Prep time: 20 minutes | Cook time: 15 minutes | Serves 2

2 snapper fillets
1 shallot, peeled and sliced
2 garlic cloves, halved
1 bell pepper, sliced
1 small-sized serrano pepper, sliced
1 tomato, sliced
1 tablespoon olive oil
¼ teaspoon freshly ground black pepper
½ teaspoon paprika
Sea salt, to taste
2 bay leaves

Place two baking paper sheets on a working surface. Place the fish in the center of one side of the baking paper. Top with the shallot, garlic, peppers, and tomato. Drizzle olive oil over the fish and vegetables. Season with black pepper, paprika, and salt. Add the bay leaves. Fold over the other half of the baking paper. Now, fold the paper around the edges tightly and create a half moon shape, sealing the fish inside. Cook in the preheated air fryer at 200°C for 15 minutes. Serve warm.

Tuna Patty Sliders

Prep time: 15 minutes | Cook time: 10 to 15 minutes | Serves 4

3 cans tuna, 140 g each, packed in water
40 g whole-wheat panko bread crumbs
50 g shredded Parmesan cheese
1 tablespoon Sriracha
¾ teaspoon black pepper
10 whole-wheat buns
Cooking spray

Preheat the air fryer to 176°C. Spray the air fryer basket lightly with cooking spray. In a medium bowl combine the tuna, bread crumbs, Parmesan cheese, Sriracha, and black pepper and stir to combine. Form the mixture into 10 patties. Place the patties in the air fryer basket in a single layer. Spray the patties lightly with cooking spray. You may need to cook them in batches. Air fry for 6 to 8 minutes. Turn the patties over and lightly spray with cooking spray. Air fry until golden brown and crisp, another 4 to 7 more minutes. Serve warm.

New Orleans-Style Crab Cakes

Prep time: 10 minutes | Cook time: 8 to 10 minutes | Serves 4

190 g bread crumbs
2 teaspoons Creole Seasoning
1 teaspoon dry mustard
1 teaspoon salt
1 teaspoon freshly ground black pepper
360 g crab meat
2 large eggs, beaten
1 teaspoon butter, melted
⅓ cup minced onion
Cooking spray
Tartar Sauce, for serving

Preheat the air fryer to 176°C. Line the air fryer basket with baking paper. In a medium bowl, whisk the bread crumbs, Creole Seasoning, dry mustard, salt, and pepper until blended. Add the crab meat, eggs, butter, and onion. Stir until blended. Shape the crab mixture into 8 patties. Place the crab cakes on the baking paper and spritz with oil. Air fry for 4 minutes. Flip the cakes, spritz them with oil, and air fry for 4 to 6 minutes more until the outsides are firm and a fork inserted into the center comes out clean. Serve with the Tartar Sauce.

Crispy Fish Sticks

Prep time: 15 minutes | Cook time: 10 minutes | Serves 4

30 g crushed panko breadcrumbs
25 g blanched finely ground almond flour
½ teaspoon Old Bay seasoning
1 tablespoon coconut oil
1 large egg
455 g cod fillet, cut into ¾-inch strips

Place panko, almond flour, Old Bay seasoning, and coconut oil into a large bowl and mix together. In a medium bowl, whisk egg. Dip each fish stick into the egg and then gently press into the flour mixture, coating as fully and evenly as possible. Place fish sticks into the air fryer basket. Adjust the temperature to 204°C and air fry for 10 minutes or until golden. Serve immediately.

Tuna-Stuffed Tomatoes

Prep time: 5 minutes | Cook time: 5 minutes | Serves 2

2 medium beefsteak tomatoes, tops removed, seeded, membranes removed
2 (75 g) g tuna fillets packed in water, drained
1 medium stalk celery, trimmed and chopped
2 tablespoons mayonnaise
¼ teaspoon salt
¼ teaspoon ground black pepper
2 teaspoons coconut oil
25 g shredded mild Cheddar cheese

Scoop pulp out of each tomato, leaving ½-inch shell. In a medium bowl, mix tuna, celery, mayonnaise, salt, and pepper. Drizzle with coconut oil. Spoon ½ mixture into each tomato and top each with 2 tablespoons Cheddar. Place tomatoes into ungreased air fryer basket. Adjust the temperature to 160°C and air fry for 5 minutes. Cheese will be melted when done. Serve warm.

Parmesan Lobster Tails

Prep time: 5 minutes | Cook time: 7 minutes | Serves 4

4 (110 g) lobster tails	¼ teaspoon salt
2 tablespoons salted butter, melted	¼ teaspoon ground black pepper
1½ teaspoons Cajun seasoning, divided	40 g grated Parmesan cheese
	15 g pork scratchings, finely crushed

Cut lobster tails open carefully with a pair of scissors and gently pull meat away from shells, resting meat on top of shells. Brush lobster meat with butter and sprinkle with 1 teaspoon Cajun seasoning, ¼ teaspoon per tail. In a small bowl, mix remaining Cajun seasoning, salt and pepper, Parmesan, and pork scratchings. Gently press ¼ mixture onto meat on each lobster tail. Carefully place tails into ungreased air fryer basket. Adjust the temperature to 204°C and air fry for 7 minutes. Lobster tails will be crispy and golden on top and have an internal temperature of at least 64°C when done. Serve warm.

Mediterranean-Style Cod

Prep time: 5 minutes | Cook time: 12 minutes | Serves 4

4 cod fillets, 170 g each	6 cherry tomatoes, halved
3 tablespoons fresh lemon juice	45 g pitted and sliced kalamata olives
1 tablespoon olive oil	
¼ teaspoon salt	

Place cod into an ungreased round nonstick baking dish. Pour lemon juice into dish and drizzle cod with olive oil. Sprinkle with salt. Place tomatoes and olives around baking dish in between fillets. Place dish into air fryer basket. Adjust the temperature to 176°C and bake for 12 minutes, carefully turning cod halfway through cooking. Fillets will be lightly browned, easily flake, and have an internal temperature of at least 64°C when done. Serve warm.

Mouthwatering Cod over Creamy Leek Noodles

Prep time: 10 minutes | Cook time: 24 minutes | Serves 4

1 small leek, sliced into long thin noodles	20 g grated Parmesan cheese
120 ml heavy cream	2 tablespoons mayonnaise
2 cloves garlic, minced	2 tablespoons unsalted butter, softened
1 teaspoon fine sea salt, divided	1 tablespoon chopped fresh thyme, or ½ teaspoon dried thyme leaves, plus more for garnish
4 cod fillets, 110 g each (about 1 inch thick)	
½ teaspoon ground black pepper	
Coating:	

Preheat the air fryer to 176°C. Place the leek noodles in a casserole dish or a pan that will fit in your air fryer. In a small bowl, stir together the cream, garlic, and ½ teaspoon of the salt. Pour the mixture over the leeks and cook in the air fryer for 10 minutes, or until the leeks are very tender. Pat the fish dry and season with the remaining ½ teaspoon of salt and the pepper. When the leeks are ready, open the air fryer and place the fish fillets on top of the leeks. Air fry for 8 to 10 minutes, until the fish flakes easily with a fork (the thicker the fillets, the longer this will take). While the fish cooks, make the coating: In a small bowl, combine the Parmesan, mayo, butter, and thyme. When the fish is ready, remove it from the air fryer and increase the heat to 218°C (or as high as your air fryer can go). Spread the fillets with a ½-inch-thick to ¾-inch-thick layer of the coating. Place the fish back in the air fryer and air fry for 3 to 4 minutes, until the coating browns. Garnish with fresh or dried thyme, if desired. Store leftovers in an airtight container in the refrigerator for up to 3 days. Reheat in a casserole dish in a preheated 176°C air fryer for 6 minutes, or until heated through.

Almond-Crusted Fish

Prep time: 15 minutes | Cook time: 10 minutes | Serves 4

4 firm white fish fillets, 110g each	Salt and pepper, to taste
45 g breadcrumbs	940 g plain flour
20 g slivered almonds, crushed	1 egg, beaten with 1 tablespoon water
2 tablespoons lemon juice	Olive or vegetable oil for misting or cooking spray
⅛ teaspoon cayenne	

Split fish fillets lengthwise down the center to create 8 pieces. Mix breadcrumbs and almonds together and set aside. Mix the lemon juice and cayenne together. Brush on all sides of fish. Season fish to taste with salt and pepper. Place the flour on a sheet of wax paper. Roll fillets in flour, dip in egg wash, and roll in the crumb mixture. Mist both sides of fish with oil or cooking spray. Spray the air fryer basket and lay fillets inside. Roast at 200°C for 5 minutes, turn fish over, and cook for an additional 5 minutes or until fish is done and flakes easily.

Fish Taco Bowl

Prep time: 10 minutes | Cook time: 12 minutes | Serves 4

½ teaspoon salt	cabbage
¼ teaspoon garlic powder	735 g mayonnaise
¼ teaspoon ground cumin	¼ teaspoon ground black pepper
4 cod fillets, 110 g each	20 g chopped pickled jalapeños
360 g finely shredded green	

Sprinkle salt, garlic powder, and cumin over cod and place into ungreased air fryer basket. Adjust the temperature to 176°C and air fry for 12 minutes, turning fillets halfway through cooking. Cod will flake easily and have an internal temperature of at least 64°C when done. In a large bowl, toss cabbage with mayonnaise, pepper, and jalapeños until fully coated. Serve cod warm over cabbage slaw on four medium plates.

Honey-Glazed Salmon

Prep time: 5 minutes | Cook time: 12 minutes | Serves 4

60 ml raw honey
4 garlic cloves, minced
1 tablespoon olive oil

½ teaspoon salt
Olive oil cooking spray
4 (1½-inch-thick) salmon fillets

Preheat the air fryer to 192°C. In a small bowl, mix together the honey, garlic, olive oil, and salt. Spray the bottom of the air fryer basket with olive oil cooking spray, and place the salmon in a single layer on the bottom of the air fryer basket. Brush the top of each fillet with the honey-garlic mixture, and roast for 10 to 12 minutes, or until the internal temperature reaches 64°C.

Air Fryer Fish Fry

Prep time: 5 minutes | Cook time: 15 minutes | Serves 4

470 ml low-fat buttermilk
½ teaspoon garlic powder
½ teaspoon onion powder
4 (110 g) sole fillets

70 g plain yellow cornmeal
45 g chickpea flour
¼ teaspoon cayenne pepper
Freshly ground black pepper

In a large bowl, combine the buttermilk, garlic powder, and onion powder. Add the sole, turning until well coated, and set aside to marinate for 20 minutes. In a shallow bowl, stir the cornmeal, chickpea flour, cayenne, and pepper together. Dredge the fillets in the meal mixture, turning until well coated. Place in the basket of an air fryer. Set the air fryer to 192°C, close, and cook for 12 minutes.

Crunchy Air Fried Cod Fillets

Prep time: 10 minutes | Cook time: 12 minutes | Serves 2

40 g panko bread crumbs
1 teaspoon vegetable oil
1 small shallot, minced
1 small garlic clove, minced
½ teaspoon minced fresh thyme
Salt and pepper, to taste
1 tablespoon minced fresh parsley

1 tablespoon mayonnaise
1 large egg yolk
¼ teaspoon grated lemon zest, plus lemon wedges for serving
2 (230 g) skinless cod fillets, 1¼ inches thick
Vegetable oil spray

Preheat the air fryer to 150°C. Make foil sling for air fryer basket by folding 1 long sheet of aluminum foil so it is 4 inches wide. Lay sheet of foil widthwise across basket, pressing foil into and up sides of basket. Fold excess foil as needed so that edges of foil are flush with top of basket. Lightly spray the foil and basket with vegetable oil spray. Toss the panko with the oil in a bowl until evenly coated. Stir in the shallot, garlic, thyme, ¼ teaspoon salt, and ⅛ teaspoon pepper. Microwave, stirring frequently, until the panko is light golden brown, about 2 minutes. Transfer to a shallow dish and let cool slightly; stir in the parsley. Whisk the mayonnaise, egg yolk, lemon zest, and ⅛ teaspoon pepper together in another bowl. Pat the cod dry with paper towels and season with salt and pepper.

Arrange the fillets, skinned-side down, on plate and brush tops evenly with mayonnaise mixture. (Tuck thinner tail ends of fillets under themselves as needed to create uniform pieces.) Working with 1 fillet at a time, dredge the coated side in panko mixture, pressing gently to adhere. Arrange the fillets, crumb-side up, on sling in the prepared basket, spaced evenly apart. Bake for 12 to 16 minutes, using a sling to rotate fillets halfway through cooking. Using a sling, carefully remove cod from air fryer. Serve with the lemon wedges.

Chilean Sea Bass with Olive Relish

Prep time: 10 minutes | Cook time: 10 minutes | Serves 2

Olive oil spray
2 (170 g) Chilean sea bass fillets or other firm-fleshed white fish
3 tablespoons extra-virgin olive oil
½ teaspoon ground cumin

½ teaspoon kosher or coarse sea salt
½ teaspoon black pepper
60 g pitted green olives, diced
10 g finely diced onion
1 teaspoon chopped capers

Spray the air fryer basket with the olive oil spray. Drizzle the fillets with the olive oil and sprinkle with the cumin, salt, and pepper. Place the fish in the air fryer basket. Set the air fryer to 164°C for 10 minutes, or until the fish flakes easily with a fork. Meanwhile, in a small bowl, stir together the olives, onion, and capers. Serve the fish topped with the relish.

Baked Salmon with Tomatoes and Olives

Prep time: 5 minutes | Cook time: 8 minutes | Serves 4

2 tablespoons olive oil
4 (1½-inch-thick) salmon fillets
½ teaspoon salt
¼ teaspoon cayenne

1 teaspoon chopped fresh dill
2 plum tomatoes, diced
45 g sliced Kalamata olives
4 lemon slices

Preheat the air fryer to 192°C. Brush the olive oil on both sides of the salmon fillets, and then season them lightly with salt, cayenne, and dill. Place the fillets in a single layer in the basket of the air fryer, then layer the tomatoes and olives over the top. Top each fillet with a lemon slice. Bake for 8 minutes, or until the salmon has reached an internal temperature of 64°C.

Tuna Steak

Prep time: 10 minutes | Cook time: 12 minutes | Serves 4

455 g tuna steaks, boneless and cubed
1 tablespoon mustard

1 tablespoon avocado oil
1 tablespoon apple cider vinegar

Mix avocado oil with mustard and apple cider vinegar. Then brush tuna steaks with mustard mixture and put in the air fryer basket. Cook the fish at 182°C for 6 minutes per side.

Marinated Swordfish Skewers

Prep time: 30 minutes | Cook time: 6 to 8 minutes | Serves 4

455 g filleted swordfish
60 ml avocado oil
2 tablespoons freshly squeezed lemon juice
1 tablespoon minced fresh parsley
2 teaspoons Dijon mustard
Sea salt and freshly ground black pepper, to taste
85 g cherry tomatoes

Cut the fish into 1½-inch chunks, picking out any remaining bones. In a large bowl, whisk together the oil, lemon juice, parsley, and Dijon mustard. Season to taste with salt and pepper. Add the fish and toss to coat the pieces. Cover and marinate the fish chunks in the refrigerator for 30 minutes. Remove the fish from the marinade. Thread the fish and cherry tomatoes on 4 skewers, alternating as you go. Set the air fryer to 204°C. Place the skewers in the air fryer basket and air fry for 3 minutes. Flip the skewers and cook for 3 to 5 minutes longer, until the fish is cooked through and an instant-read thermometer reads 60°C.

Panko Crab Sticks with Mayo Sauce

Prep time: 5 minutes | Cook time: 12 minutes | Serves 4

Crab Sticks: Cooking spray
2 eggs   Mayo Sauce:
120 g plain flour   115 g mayonnaise
50 g panko bread crumbs   1 lime, juiced
1 tablespoon Old Bay seasoning 2 garlic cloves, minced
455 g crab sticks

Preheat air fryer to 200°C. In a bowl, beat the eggs. In a shallow bowl, place the flour. In another shallow bowl, thoroughly combine the panko bread crumbs and old bay seasoning. Dredge the crab sticks in the flour, shaking off any excess, then in the beaten eggs, finally press them in the bread crumb mixture to coat well. Arrange the crab sticks in the air fryer basket and spray with cooking spray. Air fry for 12 minutes until golden brown. Flip the crab sticks halfway through the cooking time. Meanwhile, make the sauce by whisking together the mayo, lime juice, and garlic in a small bowl. Serve the crab sticks with the mayo sauce on the side.

Apple Cider Mussels

Prep time: 10 minutes | Cook time: 2 minutes | Serves 5

900 g mussels, cleaned and de-   1 teaspoon ground cumin
bearded   1 tablespoon avocado oil
1 teaspoon onion powder   60 ml apple cider vinegar

Mix mussels with onion powder, ground cumin, avocado oil, and apple cider vinegar. Put the mussels in the air fryer and cook at 202°C for 2 minutes.

Golden Prawns

Prep time: 20 minutes | Cook time: 7 minutes | Serves 4

2 egg whites   1 teaspoon garlic powder
60 g coconut flour   ½ teaspoon dried rosemary
120 g Parmigiano-Reggiano,   ½ teaspoon sea salt
grated   ½ teaspoon ground black pepper
½ teaspoon celery seeds   680 g prawns, peeled and
½ teaspoon porcini powder   deveined
½ teaspoon onion powder

Whisk the egg with coconut flour and Parmigiano-Reggiano. Add in seasonings and mix to combine well. Dip your prawns in the batter. Roll until they are covered on all sides. Cook in the preheated air fryer at 200°C for 5 to 7 minutes or until golden brown. Work in batches. Serve with lemon wedges if desired.

Tuna and Fruit Kebabs

Prep time: 15 minutes | Cook time: 8 to 12 minutes | Serves 4

455 g tuna steaks, cut into 1-inch   1 tablespoon honey
cubes   2 teaspoons grated fresh ginger
85 g canned pineapple chunks,   1 teaspoon olive oil
drained, juice reserved   Pinch cayenne pepper
75 g large red grapes

Thread the tuna, pineapple, and grapes on 8 bamboo or 4 metal skewers that fit in the air fryer. In a small bowl, whisk the honey, 1 tablespoon of reserved pineapple juice, the ginger, olive oil, and cayenne. Brush this mixture over the kebabs. Let them stand for 10 minutes. Air fry the kebabs at 188°C for 8 to 12 minutes, or until the tuna reaches an internal temperature of at least 64°C on a meat thermometer, and the fruit is tender and glazed, brushing once with the remaining sauce. Discard any remaining marinade. Serve immediately.

Tilapia Almondine

Prep time: 10 minutes | Cook time: 10 minutes | Serves 2

50 g almond flour or fine dried   salt
bread crumbs   60 g mayonnaise
2 tablespoons salted butter or   2 tilapia fillets
ghee, melted   435 g thinly sliced almonds
1 teaspoon black pepper   Vegetable oil spray
½ teaspoon kosher or coarse sea

In a small bowl, mix together the almond flour, butter, pepper and salt. Spread the mayonnaise on both sides of each fish fillet. Dredge the fillets in the almond flour mixture. Spread the sliced almonds on one side of each fillet, pressing lightly to adhere. Spray the air fryer basket with vegetable oil spray. Place the fish fillets in the basket. Set the air fryer to 164°C for 10 minutes, or until the fish flakes easily with a fork.

Lemon-Pepper Trout

Prep time: 5 minutes | Cook time: 15 minutes | Serves 4

4 trout fillets
2 tablespoons olive oil
½ teaspoon salt
1 teaspoon black pepper

2 garlic cloves, sliced
1 lemon, sliced, plus additional wedges for serving

Preheat the air fryer to 192°C. Brush each fillet with olive oil on both sides and season with salt and pepper. Place the fillets in an even layer in the air fryer basket. Place the sliced garlic over the tops of the trout fillets, then top the garlic with lemon slices and roast for 12 to 15 minutes, or until it has reached an internal temperature of 64°C. Serve with fresh lemon wedges.

Snapper with Fruit

Prep time: 15 minutes | Cook time: 9 to 13 minutes | Serves 4

4 red snapper fillets, 100 g each
2 teaspoons olive oil
3 nectarines, halved and pitted
3 plums, halved and pitted
150 g red grapes

1 tablespoon freshly squeezed lemon juice
1 tablespoon honey
½ teaspoon dried thyme

Put the red snapper in the air fryer basket and drizzle with the olive oil. Air fry at 200°C for 4 minutes. Remove the basket and add the nectarines and plums. Scatter the grapes over all. Drizzle with the lemon juice and honey and sprinkle with the thyme. Return the basket to the air fryer and air fry for 5 to 9 minutes more, or until the fish flakes when tested with a fork and the fruit is tender. Serve immediately.

Lemon-Tarragon Fish en Papillote

Prep time: 10 minutes | Cook time: 15 minutes | Serves 2

2 tablespoons salted butter, melted
1 tablespoon fresh lemon juice
½ teaspoon dried tarragon, crushed, or 2 sprigs fresh tarragon
1 teaspoon kosher or coarse sea salt
85 g julienned carrots

435 g julienned fennel, or 1 stalk julienned celery
75 g thinly sliced red bell pepper
2 cod fillets, 170 g each, thawed if frozen
Vegetable oil spray
½ teaspoon black pepper

In a medium bowl, combine the butter, lemon juice, tarragon, and ½ teaspoon of the salt. Whisk well until you get a creamy sauce. Add the carrots, fennel, and bell pepper and toss to combine; set aside. Cut two squares of baking paper each large enough to hold one fillet and half the vegetables. Spray the fillets with vegetable oil spray. Season both sides with the remaining ½ teaspoon salt and the black pepper. Lay one fillet down on each baking paper square. Top

each with half the vegetables. Pour any remaining sauce over the vegetables. Fold over the baking paper and crimp the sides in small, tight folds to hold the fish, vegetables, and sauce securely inside the packet. Place the packets in the air fryer basket. Set the air fryer to 176°C for 15 minutes. Transfer each packet to a plate. Cut open with scissors just before serving (be careful, as the steam inside will be hot).

Trout Amandine with Lemon Butter Sauce

Prep time: 20 minutes | Cook time:8 minutes | Serves 4

Trout Amandine:
65 g toasted almonds
30 g grated Parmesan cheese
1 teaspoon salt
½ teaspoon freshly ground black pepper
2 tablespoons butter, melted
4 trout fillets, or salmon fillets, 110 g each
Cooking spray

Lemon Butter Sauce:
8 tablespoons butter, melted
2 tablespoons freshly squeezed lemon juice
½ teaspoon Worcestershire sauce
½ teaspoon salt
½ teaspoon freshly ground black pepper
¼ teaspoon hot sauce

In a blender or food processor, pulse the almonds for 5 to 10 seconds until finely processed. Transfer to a shallow bowl and whisk in the Parmesan cheese, salt, and pepper. Place the melted butter in another shallow bowl. One at a time, dip the fish in the melted butter, then the almond mixture, coating thoroughly. Preheat the air fryer to 150°C. Line the air fryer basket with baking paper. Place the coated fish on the baking paper and spritz with oil. Bake for 4 minutes. Flip the fish, spritz it with oil, and bake for 4 minutes more until the fish flakes easily with a fork. In a small bowl, whisk the butter, lemon juice, Worcestershire sauce, salt, pepper, and hot sauce until blended. Serve with the fish.

Baked Monkfish

Prep time: 20 minutes | Cook time: 12 minutes | Serves 2

2 teaspoons olive oil
100 g celery, sliced
2 bell peppers, sliced
1 teaspoon dried thyme
½ teaspoon dried marjoram
½ teaspoon dried rosemary
2 monkfish fillets
1 tablespoon coconut aminos, or

tamari
2 tablespoons lime juice
Coarse salt and ground black pepper, to taste
1 teaspoon cayenne pepper
90 g Kalamata olives, pitted and sliced

In a nonstick skillet, heat the olive oil for 1 minute. Once hot, sauté the celery and peppers until tender, about 4 minutes. Sprinkle with thyme, marjoram, and rosemary and set aside. Toss the fish fillets with the coconut aminos, lime juice, salt, black pepper, and cayenne pepper. Place the fish fillets in the lightly greased air fryer basket and bake at 200°C for 8 minutes. Turn them over, add the olives, and cook an additional 4 minutes. Serve with the sautéed vegetables on the side. Bon appétit!

Prawn Bake

Prep time: 15 minutes | Cook time: 5 minutes | Serves 4

400 g prawns, peeled and deveined
1 egg, beaten
120 ml coconut milk

120 g Cheddar cheese, shredded
½ teaspoon coconut oil
1 teaspoon ground coriander

In the mixing bowl, mix prawns with egg, coconut milk, Cheddar cheese, coconut oil, and ground coriander. Then put the mixture in the baking ramekins and put in the air fryer. Cook the prawns at 204°C for 5 minutes.

Seasoned Tuna Steaks

Prep time: 5 minutes | Cook time: 9 minutes | Serves 4

1 teaspoon garlic powder
½ teaspoon salt
¼ teaspoon dried thyme
¼ teaspoon dried oregano

4 tuna steaks
2 tablespoons olive oil
1 lemon, quartered

Preheat the air fryer to 192°C. In a small bowl, whisk together the garlic powder, salt, thyme, and oregano. Coat the tuna steaks with olive oil. Season both sides of each steak with the seasoning blend. Place the steaks in a single layer in the air fryer basket. Roast for 5 minutes, then flip and roast for an additional 3 to 4 minutes.

Southern-Style Catfish

Prep time: 10 minutes | Cook time: 12 minutes | Serves 4

4 (200 g) catfish fillets
80 ml heavy whipping cream
1 tablespoon lemon juice
110 g blanched finely ground almond flour

2 teaspoons Old Bay seasoning
½ teaspoon salt
¼ teaspoon ground black pepper

Place catfish fillets into a large bowl with cream and pour in lemon juice. Stir to coat. In a separate large bowl, mix flour and Old Bay seasoning. Remove each fillet and gently shake off excess cream. Sprinkle with salt and pepper. Press each fillet gently into flour mixture on both sides to coat. Place fillets into ungreased air fryer basket. Adjust the temperature to 204°C and air fry for 12 minutes, turning fillets halfway through cooking. Catfish will be golden brown and have an internal temperature of at least 64°C when done. Serve warm.

Chapter 5 Beef, Pork, and Lamb

Chapter 5 Beef, Pork, and Lamb

Roast Beef with Horseradish Cream

Prep time: 5 minutes | Cook time: 35 to 45 minutes | Serves 6

900 g beef roasting joint
1 tablespoon salt
2 teaspoons garlic powder
1 teaspoon freshly ground black pepper
1 teaspoon dried thyme
Horseradish Cream:

80 ml double cream
80 ml sour cream
80 ml grated horseradish
2 teaspoons fresh lemon juice
Salt and freshly ground black pepper, to taste

Preheat the air fryer to 204°C. Season the beef with the salt, garlic powder, black pepper, and thyme. Place the beef fat-side down in the basket of the air fryer and lightly coat with olive oil. Pausing halfway through the cooking time to turn the meat, air fry for 35 to 45 minutes, until a thermometer inserted into the thickest part indicates the desired doneness, 52°C (rare) to 64°C (medium). Let the beef rest for 10 minutes before slicing. To make the horseradish cream: In a small bowl, combine the double cream, sour cream, horseradish, and lemon juice. Whisk until thoroughly combined. Season to taste with salt and freshly ground black pepper. Serve alongside the beef.

Beef Mince Taco Rolls

Prep time: 20 minutes | Cook time: 10 minutes | Serves 4

230 g 80/20 beef mince
80 ml water
1 tablespoon chili powder
2 teaspoons cumin
½ teaspoon garlic powder
¼ teaspoon dried oregano
60 ml tinned diced tomatoes

2 tablespoons chopped coriander
355 ml shredded Mozzarella cheese
120 ml blanched finely ground almond flour
60 g full-fat cream cheese
1 large egg

In a medium skillet over medium heat, brown the beef mince about 7 to 10 minutes. When meat is fully cooked, drain. Add water to skillet and stir in chili powder, cumin, garlic powder, oregano, and tomatoes. Add coriander. Bring to a boil, then reduce heat to simmer for 3 minutes. In a large microwave-safe bowl, place Mozzarella, almond flour, cream cheese, and egg. Microwave for 1 minute. Stir the mixture quickly until smooth ball of dough forms. Cut a piece of parchment for your work surface. Press the dough into a large rectangle on the parchment, wetting your hands to prevent the dough from sticking as necessary. Cut the dough into eight rectangles. On each rectangle place a few spoons of the meat mixture. Fold the short ends of each roll toward the center and roll the length as you would a burrito. Cut a piece of parchment to fit your air fryer basket. Place taco rolls onto the parchment and place into the air fryer basket. Adjust the temperature to 182°C and air fry for 10 minutes. Flip halfway through the cooking time. Allow to cool 10 minutes before serving.

Spicy Lamb Sirloin Chops

Prep time: 30 minutes | Cook time: 15 minutes | Serves 4

½ brown onion, coarsely chopped
4 coin-size slices peeled fresh ginger
5 garlic cloves
1 teaspoon garam masala
1 teaspoon ground fennel

1 teaspoon ground cinnamon
1 teaspoon ground turmeric
½ to 1 teaspoon cayenne pepper
½ teaspoon ground cardamom
1 teaspoon coarse or flaky salt
450 g lamb sirloin chops

In a blender, combine the onion, ginger, garlic, garam masala, fennel, cinnamon, turmeric, cayenne, cardamom, and salt. Pulse until the onion is finely minced and the mixture forms a thick paste, 3 to 4 minutes. Place the lamb chops in a large bowl. Slash the meat and fat with a sharp knife several times to allow the marinade to penetrate better. Add the spice paste to the bowl and toss the lamb to coat. Marinate at room temperature for 30 minutes or cover and refrigerate for up to 24 hours. Place the lamb chops in a single layer in the air fryer basket. Set the air fryer to 164°C for 15 minutes, turning the chops halfway through the cooking time. Use a meat thermometer to ensure the lamb has reached an internal temperature of 64°C (medium-rare).

Beefy Poppers

Prep time: 15 minutes | Cook time: 15 minutes | Makes 8 poppers

8 medium jalapeño peppers, stemmed, halved, and seeded
1 (230 g) package cream cheese (or cream cheese style spread for dairy-free), softened
900 g beef mince (85% lean)

1 teaspoon fine sea salt
½ teaspoon ground black pepper
8 slices thin-cut bacon
Fresh coriander leaves, for garnish

Spray the air fryer basket with avocado oil. Preheat the air fryer to 204°C. Stuff each jalapeño half with a few tablespoons of cream cheese. Place the halves back together again to form 8 jalapeños. Season the beef mince with the salt and pepper and mix with your hands to incorporate. Flatten about 110 g of beef in the palm of your hand and place a stuffed jalapeño in the center. Fold the beef around the jalapeño, forming an egg shape. Wrap the beef-covered jalapeño with a slice of bacon and secure it with a toothpick. Place the jalapeños in the air fryer basket, leaving space between them (if you're using a smaller air fryer, work in batches if necessary), and air fry for 15 minutes, or until the beef is cooked through and the bacon is crispy. Garnish with coriander before serving. Store leftovers in an airtight container in the fridge for 3 days or in the freezer for up to a month. Reheat in a preheated 176°C air fryer for 4 minutes, or until heated through and the bacon is crispy.

Blue Cheese Steak Salad

Prep time: 30 minutes | Cook time: 22 minutes | Serves 4

2 tablespoons balsamic vinegar
2 tablespoons red wine vinegar
1 tablespoon Dijon mustard
1 tablespoon granulated sweetener
1 teaspoon minced garlic
Sea salt and freshly ground black pepper, to taste

180 ml extra-virgin olive oil
450 g boneless rump steak
Avocado oil spray
1 small red onion, cut into ¼-inch-thick rounds
170 g baby spinach
120 ml cherry tomatoes, halved
85 g blue cheese, crumbled

In a blender, combine the balsamic vinegar, red wine vinegar, Dijon mustard, sweetener, and garlic. Season with salt and pepper and process until smooth. With the blender running, drizzle in the olive oil. Process until well combined. Transfer to a jar with a tight-fitting lid, and refrigerate until ready to serve (it will keep for up to 2 weeks). Season the steak with salt and pepper and let sit at room temperature for at least 45 minutes, time permitting. Set the air fryer to 204°C. Spray the steak with oil and place it in the air fryer basket. Air fry for 6 minutes. Flip the steak and spray it with more oil. Air fry for 6 minutes more for medium-rare or until the steak is done to your liking. Transfer the steak to a plate, tent with a piece of aluminum foil, and allow it to rest. Spray the onion slices with oil and place them in the air fryer basket. Cook at 204°C for 5 minutes. Flip the onion slices and spray them with more oil. Air fry for 5 minutes more. Slice the steak diagonally into thin strips. Place the spinach, cherry tomatoes, onion slices, and steak in a large bowl. Toss with the desired amount of dressing. Sprinkle with crumbled blue cheese and serve.

Mozzarella Stuffed Beef and Pork Meatballs

Prep time: 15 minutes | Cook time: 12 minutes | Serves 4 to 6

1 tablespoon olive oil
1 small onion, finely chopped
1 to 2 cloves garlic, minced
340 g beef mince
340 g pork mince
180 ml bread crumbs
60 ml grated Parmesan cheese
60 ml finely chopped fresh parsley

½ teaspoon dried oregano
1½ teaspoons salt
Freshly ground black pepper, to taste
2 eggs, lightly beaten
140 g low-moisture Mozzarella or other melting cheese, cut into 1-inch cubes

Preheat a skillet over medium-high heat. Add the oil and cook the onion and garlic until tender, but not browned. Transfer the onion and garlic to a large bowl and add the beef, pork, bread crumbs, Parmesan cheese, parsley, oregano, salt, pepper and eggs. Mix well until all the ingredients are combined. Divide the mixture into 12 evenly sized balls. Make one meatball at a time, by pressing a hole in the meatball mixture with the finger and pushing a piece of Mozzarella cheese into the hole. Mold the meat back into a ball, enclosing the cheese. Preheat the air fryer to 192°C. Working in two batches, transfer six of the meatballs to the air fryer basket and air fry for 12 minutes, shaking the basket and turning the meatballs twice during the cooking process. Repeat with the remaining 6 meatballs. Serve warm.

Garlic Balsamic London Broil

Prep time: 30 minutes | Cook time: 8 to 10 minutes | Serves 8

900 g bavette or skirt steak
3 large garlic cloves, minced
3 tablespoons balsamic vinegar
3 tablespoons wholegrain mustard

2 tablespoons olive oil
Sea salt and ground black pepper, to taste
½ teaspoon dried hot red pepper flakes

Score both sides of the cleaned steak. Thoroughly combine the remaining ingredients; massage this mixture into the meat to coat it on all sides. Let it marinate for at least 3 hours. Set the air fryer to 204°C; Then cook the steak for 15 minutes. Flip it over and cook another 10 to 12 minutes. Bon appétit!

Beef Whirls

Prep time: 30 minutes | Cook time: 18 minutes | Serves 6

3 minute steaks (170 g each)
1 (450 g) bottle Italian dressing
235 ml Italian-style bread crumbs (or plain bread crumbs with Italian seasoning to taste)
120 ml grated Parmesan cheese

1 teaspoon dried basil
1 teaspoon dried oregano
1 teaspoon dried parsley
60 ml beef stock
1 to 2 tablespoons oil

In a large resealable bag, combine the steaks and Italian dressing. Seal the bag and refrigerate to marinate for 2 hours. In a medium bowl, whisk the bread crumbs, cheese, basil, oregano, and parsley until blended. Stir in the beef stock. Place the steaks on a cutting board and cut each in half so you have 6 equal pieces. Sprinkle with the bread crumb mixture. Roll up the steaks, jelly roll-style, and secure with toothpicks. Preheat the air fryer to 204°C. Place 3 roll-ups in the air fryer basket. Cook for 5 minutes. Flip the roll-ups and spritz with oil. Cook for 4 minutes more until the internal temperature reaches 64°C. Repeat with the remaining roll-ups. Let rest for 5 to 10 minutes before serving.

Mexican Pork Chops

Prep time: 5 minutes | Cook time: 15 minutes | Serves 2

¼ teaspoon dried oregano
1½ teaspoons taco seasoning or fajita seasoning mix

2 (110 g) boneless pork chops
2 tablespoons unsalted butter, divided

Preheat the air fryer to 204°C. Combine the dried oregano and taco seasoning in a small bowl and rub the mixture into the pork chops. Brush the chops with 1 tablespoon butter. In the air fryer, air fry the chops for 15 minutes, turning them over halfway through to air fry on the other side. When the chops are a brown color, check the internal temperature has reached 64°C and remove from the air fryer. Serve with a garnish of remaining butter.

Sausage and Courgette Lasagna

Prep time: 25 minutes | Cook time: 56 minutes | Serves 4

1 courgette
Avocado oil spray
170 g hot Italian-seasoned sausage, casings removed
60 g mushrooms, stemmed and sliced
1 teaspoon minced garlic
235 ml keto-friendly marinara sauce

180 ml ricotta cheese
235 ml shredded gruyere cheese, divided
120 ml finely grated Parmesan cheese
Sea salt and freshly ground black pepper, to taste
Fresh basil, for garnish

Cut the courgette into long thin slices using a mandoline slicer or sharp knife. Spray both sides of the slices with oil. Place the slices in a single layer in the air fryer basket, working in batches if necessary. Set the air fryer to 164°C and air fry for 4 to 6 minutes, until most of the moisture has been released from the courgette. Place a large skillet over medium-high heat. Crumble the sausage into the hot skillet and cook for 6 minutes, breaking apart the meat with the back of a spoon. Remove the sausage from the skillet, leaving any fats that remain. Add the mushrooms to the skillet and cook for 10 minutes, until the liquid nearly evaporates. Add the garlic and cook for 1 minute more. Stir in the marinara and cook for 2 more minutes. In a medium bowl, combine the ricotta cheese, 120 ml of gruyere cheese, Parmesan cheese, and salt and pepper to taste. Spread 60 ml of the meat sauce in the bottom of a deep pan (or other pan that fits inside your air fryer). Top with half of the courgette slices. Add half of the cheese mixture. Top the cheese with half of the remaining meat sauce. Layer the remaining courgette over the meat sauce and top with the remaining cheese mixture. Top the lasagna with the remaining 120 ml of fontina cheese. Cover the lasagna with aluminum foil or parchment paper and place it in the air fryer. Bake for 25 minutes. Remove the foil and cook for 8 to 10 minutes more. Allow the lasagna to rest for 15 minutes before cutting and serving. Garnish with basil.

Asian Glazed Meatballs

Prep time: 15 minutes | Cook time: 10 minutes per batch | Serves 4 to 6

1 large shallot, finely chopped
2 cloves garlic, minced
1 tablespoon grated fresh ginger
2 teaspoons fresh thyme, finely chopped
355 ml brown mushrooms, very finely chopped (a food processor works well here)
2 tablespoons soy sauce
Freshly ground black pepper, to

taste
450 g beef mince
230 g pork mince
3 egg yolks
235 ml Thai sweet chili sauce (spring roll sauce)
60 ml toasted sesame seeds
2 spring onionspring onions, sliced

Combine the shallot, garlic, ginger, thyme, mushrooms, soy sauce, freshly ground black pepper, beef and pork mince, and egg yolks in a bowl and mix the ingredients together. Gently shape the mixture into 24 balls, about the size of a golf ball. Preheat the air fryer to 192°C. Working in batches, air fry the meatballs for 8 minutes, turning the meatballs over halfway through the cooking time.

Drizzle some of the Thai sweet chili sauce on top of each meatball and return the basket to the air fryer, air frying for another 2 minutes. Reserve the remaining Thai sweet chili sauce for serving. As soon as the meatballs are done, sprinkle with toasted sesame seeds and transfer them to a serving platter. Scatter the spring onionspring onions around and serve warm.

Bone-in Pork Chops

Prep time: 5 minutes | Cook time: 10 to 12 minutes | Serves 2

450 g bone-in pork chops
1 tablespoon avocado oil
1 teaspoon smoked paprika
½ teaspoon onion granules

¼ teaspoon cayenne pepper
Sea salt and freshly ground black pepper, to taste

Brush the pork chops with the avocado oil. In a small dish, mix together the smoked paprika, onion granules, cayenne pepper, and salt and black pepper to taste. Sprinkle the seasonings over both sides of the pork chops. Set the air fryer to 204°C. Place the chops in the air fryer basket in a single layer, working in batches if necessary. Air fry for 10 to 12 minutes, until an instant-read thermometer reads 64°C at the chops' thickest point. Remove the chops from the air fryer and allow them to rest for 5 minutes before serving.

Reuben Beef Rolls with Thousand Island Sauce

Prep time: 15 minutes | Cook time: 10 minutes per batch | Makes 10 rolls

230 g cooked salt beef, chopped
120 ml drained and chopped sauerkraut
1 (230 g) package cream cheese, softened
120 ml shredded Swiss cheese
20 slices prosciutto
Cooking spray

Thousand Island Sauce:
60 ml chopped dill pickles
60 ml tomato ketchup
180 ml mayonnaise
Fresh thyme leaves, for garnish
2 tablespoons sugar
⅛ teaspoon fine sea salt
Ground black pepper, to taste

Preheat the air fryer to 204°C and spritz with cooking spray. Combine the beef, sauerkraut, cream cheese, and Swiss cheese in a large bowl. Stir to mix well. Unroll a slice of prosciutto on a clean work surface, then top with another slice of prosciutto crosswise. Scoop up 4 tablespoons of the beef mixture in the center. Fold the top slice sides over the filling as the ends of the roll, then roll up the long sides of the bottom prosciutto and make it into a roll shape. Overlap the sides by about 1 inch. Repeat with remaining filling and prosciutto. Arrange the rolls in the preheated air fryer, seam side down, and spritz with cooking spray. Air fry for 10 minutes or until golden and crispy. Flip the rolls halfway through. Work in batches to avoid overcrowding. Meanwhile, combine the ingredients for the sauce in a small bowl. Stir to mix well. Serve the rolls with the dipping sauce.

Kale and Beef Omelet

Prep time: 15 minutes | Cook time: 16 minutes | Serves 4

230 g leftover beef, coarsely chopped
2 garlic cloves, pressed
235 ml kale, torn into pieces and wilted
1 tomato, chopped
¼ teaspoon sugar

4 eggs, beaten
4 tablespoons double cream
½ teaspoon turmeric powder
Salt and ground black pepper, to taste
⅛ teaspoon ground allspice
Cooking spray

Preheat the air fryer to 182°C. Spritz four ramekins with cooking spray. Put equal amounts of each of the ingredients into each ramekin and mix well. Air fry for 16 minutes. Serve immediately.

Meat and Rice Stuffed Peppers

Prep time: 20 minutes | Cook time: 18 minutes | Serves 4

340 g lean beef mince
110 g lean pork mince
60 ml onion, minced
1 (425 g) can finely-chopped tomatoes
1 teaspoon Worcestershire sauce
1 teaspoon barbecue seasoning
1 teaspoon honey

½ teaspoon dried basil
120 ml cooked brown rice
½ teaspoon garlic powder
½ teaspoon oregano
½ teaspoon salt
2 small peppers, cut in half, stems removed, deseeded
Cooking spray

Preheat the air fryer to 182°C and spritz a baking pan with cooking spray. Arrange the beef, pork, and onion in the baking pan and bake in the preheated air fryer for 8 minutes. Break the ground meat into chunks halfway through the cooking. Meanwhile, combine the tomatoes, Worcestershire sauce, barbecue seasoning, honey, and basil in a saucepan. Stir to mix well. Transfer the cooked meat mixture to a large bowl and add the cooked rice, garlic powder, oregano, salt, and 60 ml of the tomato mixture. Stir to mix well. Stuff the pepper halves with the mixture, then arrange the pepper halves in the air fryer and air fry for 10 minutes or until the peppers are lightly charred. Serve the stuffed peppers with the remaining tomato sauce on top.

Pork Chops with Caramelized Onions

Prep time: 20 minutes | Cook time: 23 to 34 minutes | Serves 4

4 bone-in pork chops (230 g each)
1 to 2 tablespoons oil
2 tablespoons Cajun seasoning,

divided
1 brown onion, thinly sliced
1 green pepper, thinly sliced
2 tablespoons light brown sugar

Spritz the pork chops with oil. Sprinkle 1 tablespoon of Cajun seasoning on one side of the chops. Preheat the air fryer to 204°C. Line the air fryer basket with parchment paper and spritz the parchment with oil. Place 2 pork chops, spice-side up, on the paper. Cook for 4 minutes. Flip the chops, sprinkle with the remaining 1 tablespoon of Cajun seasoning, and cook for 4 to 8 minutes

more until the internal temperature reaches 64°C, depending on the chops' thickness. Remove and keep warm while you cook the remaining 2 chops. Set the chops aside. In a baking pan, combine the onion, pepper, and brown sugar, stirring until the vegetables are coated. Place the pan in the air fryer basket and cook for 4 minutes. Stir the vegetables. Cook for 3 to 6 minutes more to your desired doneness. Spoon the vegetable mixture over the chops to serve.

Jalapeño Popper Pork Chops

Prep time: 15 minutes | Cook time: 6 to 8 minutes | Serves 4

800 g bone-in, loin pork chops
Sea salt and freshly ground black pepper, to taste
170 g cream cheese, at room temperature

110 g sliced bacon, cooked and crumbled
110 g Cheddar cheese, shredded
1 jalapeño, seeded and diced
1 teaspoon garlic powder

Cut a pocket into each pork chop, lengthwise along the side, making sure not to cut it all the way through. Season the outside of the chops with salt and pepper. In a small bowl, combine the cream cheese, bacon, Cheddar cheese, jalapeño, and garlic powder. Divide this mixture among the pork chops, stuffing it into the pocket of each chop. Set the air fryer to 204°C. Place the pork chops in the air fryer basket in a single layer, working in batches if necessary. Air fry for 3 minutes. Flip the chops and cook for 3 to 5 minutes more, until an instant-read thermometer reads 64°C. Allow the chops to rest for 5 minutes, then serve warm.

Italian Steak Rolls

Prep time: 30 minutes | Cook time: 9 minutes | Serves 4

1 tablespoon vegetable oil
2 cloves garlic, minced
2 teaspoons dried Italian seasoning
1 teaspoon coarse or flaky salt
1 teaspoon black pepper
450 g bavette or skirt steak, ¼ to ½ inch thick

1 (280 g) package frozen spinach, thawed and squeezed dry
120 ml diced jarred roasted red pepper
235 ml shredded Mozzarella cheese

In a large bowl, combine the oil, garlic, Italian seasoning, salt, and pepper. Whisk to combine. Add the steak to the bowl, turning to ensure the entire steak is covered with the seasonings. Cover and marinate at room temperature for 30 minutes or in the refrigerator for up to 24 hours. Lay the steak on a flat surface. Spread the spinach evenly over the steak, leaving a ¼-inch border at the edge. Evenly top each steak with the red pepper and cheese. Starting at a long end, roll up the steak as tightly as possible, ending seam side down. Use 2 or 3 wooden toothpicks to hold the roll together. Using a sharp knife, cut the roll in half so that it better fits in the air fryer basket. Place the steak roll, seam side down, in the air fryer basket. Set the air fryer to 204°C for 9 minutes. Use a meat thermometer to ensure the steak has reached an internal temperature of 64°C. (It is critical to not overcook bavette steak, so as to not toughen the meat.) Let the steak rest for 10 minutes before cutting into slices to serve.

Chorizo and Beef Burger

Prep time: 10 minutes | Cook time: 15 minutes | Serves 4

340 g 80/20 beef mince
110 g Mexican-style chorizo crumb
60 ml chopped onion
5 slices pickled jalapeños,

chopped
2 teaspoons chili powder
1 teaspoon minced garlic
¼ teaspoon cumin

In a large bowl, mix all ingredients. Divide the mixture into four sections and form them into burger patties. Place burger patties into the air fryer basket, working in batches if necessary. Adjust the temperature to 192ºC and air fry for 15 minutes. Flip the patties halfway through the cooking time. Serve warm.

Filipino Crispy Pork Belly

Prep time: 20 minutes | Cook time: 30 minutes | Serves 4

450 g pork belly
700 ml water
6 garlic cloves
2 tablespoons soy sauce

1 teaspoon coarse or flaky salt
1 teaspoon black pepper
2 bay leaves

Cut the pork belly into three thick chunks so it will cook more evenly. Place the pork, water, garlic, soy sauce, salt, pepper, and bay leaves in the inner pot of an Instant Pot or other electric pressure cooker. Seal and cook at high pressure for 15 minutes. Let the pressure release naturally for 10 minutes, then manually release the remaining pressure. (If you do not have a pressure cooker, place all the ingredients in a large saucepan. Cover and cook over low heat until a knife can be easily inserted into the skin side of pork belly, about 1 hour.) Using tongs, very carefully transfer the meat to a wire rack over a rimmed baking sheet to drain and dry for 10 minutes. Cut each chunk of pork belly into two long slices. Arrange the slices in the air fryer basket. Set the air fryer to 204ºC for 15 minutes, or until the fat has crisped. Serve immediately.

Rack of Lamb with Pistachio Crust

Prep time: 10 minutes | Cook time: 19 minutes | Serves 2

120 ml finely chopped pistachios
3 tablespoons panko bread crumbs
1 teaspoon chopped fresh rosemary
2 teaspoons chopped fresh

oregano
Salt and freshly ground black pepper, to taste
1 tablespoon olive oil
1 rack of lamb, bones trimmed of fat and frenched
1 tablespoon Dijon mustard

Preheat the air fryer to 192ºC. Combine the pistachios, bread crumbs, rosemary, oregano, salt and pepper in a small bowl. (This is a good job for your food processor if you have one.) Drizzle in the olive oil and stir to combine. Season the rack of lamb with salt and pepper on all sides and transfer it to the air fryer basket with the fat side facing up. Air fry the lamb for 12 minutes. Remove the lamb from the air fryer and brush the fat side of the lamb rack with the Dijon mustard. Coat the rack with the pistachio mixture, pressing the bread crumbs onto the lamb with your hands and rolling the bottom of the rack in any of the crumbs that fall off. Return the rack of lamb to the air fryer and air fry for another 3 to 7 minutes or until an instant read thermometer reads 60ºC for medium. Add or subtract a couple of minutes for lamb that is more or less well cooked. (Your time will vary depending on how big the rack of lamb is.) Let the lamb rest for at least 5 minutes. Then, slice into chops and serve.

Ham Hock Mac and Cheese

Prep time: 20 minutes | Cook time: 25 minutes | Serves 4

2 large eggs, beaten
475 ml cottage cheese, full-fat or low-fat
475 ml grated sharp Cheddar cheese, divided
235 ml sour cream
½ teaspoon salt

1 teaspoon freshly ground black pepper
475 ml uncooked elbow macaroni
2 ham hocks (about 310 g each), meat removed and diced
1 to 2 tablespoons oil

In a large bowl, stir together the eggs, cottage cheese, 235 ml of the Cheddar cheese, sour cream, salt, and pepper. Stir in the macaroni and the diced meat. Preheat the air fryer to 182ºC. Spritz a baking pan with oil. Pour the macaroni mixture into the prepared pan, making sure all noodles are covered with sauce. Cook for 12 minutes. Stir in the remaining 235 ml of Cheddar cheese, making sure all the noodles are covered with sauce. Cook for 13 minutes more, until the noodles are tender. Let rest for 5 minutes before serving.

Lamb Chops with Horseradish Sauce

Prep time: 30 minutes | Cook time: 13 minutes | Serves 4

Lamb:
4 lamb loin chops
2 tablespoons vegetable oil
1 clove garlic, minced
½ teaspoon coarse or flaky salt
½ teaspoon black pepper
Horseradish Cream Sauce:

120 ml mayonnaise
1 tablespoon Dijon mustard
1 to 1½ tablespoons grated horseradish
2 teaspoons sugar
Vegetable oil spray

For the lamb: Brush the lamb chops with the oil, rub with the garlic, and sprinkle with the salt and pepper. Marinate at room temperature for 30 minutes. Meanwhile, for the sauce: In a medium bowl, combine the mayonnaise, mustard, horseradish, and sugar. Stir until well combined. Set aside half of the sauce for serving. Spray the air fryer basket with vegetable oil spray and place the chops in the basket. Set the air fryer to 164ºC for 10 minutes, turning the chops halfway through the cooking time. Remove the chops from the air fryer and add to the bowl with the horseradish sauce, turning to coat with the sauce. Place the chops back in the air fryer basket. Set the air fryer to 204ºC for 3 minutes. Use a meat thermometer to ensure the meat has reached an internal temperature of 64ºC (for medium-rare). Serve the chops with the reserved horseradish sauce.

Italian Lamb Chops with Avocado Mayo

Prep time: 5 minutes | Cook time: 12 minutes | Serves 2

2 lamp chops
2 teaspoons Italian herbs
2 avocados

120 ml mayonnaise
1 tablespoon lemon juice

Season the lamb chops with the Italian herbs, then set aside for 5 minutes. Preheat the air fryer to 204°C and place the rack inside. Put the chops on the rack and air fry for 12 minutes. In the meantime, halve the avocados and open to remove the pits. Spoon the flesh into a blender. Add the mayonnaise and lemon juice and pulse until a smooth consistency is achieved. Take care when removing the chops from the air fryer, then plate up and serve with the avocado mayo.

Cajun Bacon Pork Loin Fillet

Prep time: 30 minutes | Cook time: 20 minutes | Serves 6

680 g pork loin fillet or pork tenderloin
3 tablespoons olive oil
2 tablespoons Cajun spice mix

Salt, to taste
6 slices bacon
Olive oil spray

Cut the pork in half so that it will fit in the air fryer basket. Place both pieces of meat in a resealable plastic bag. Add the oil, Cajun seasoning, and salt to taste, if using. Seal the bag and massage to coat all of the meat with the oil and seasonings. Marinate in the refrigerator for at least 1 hour or up to 24 hours. Remove the pork from the bag and wrap 3 bacon slices around each piece. Spray the air fryer basket with olive oil spray. Place the meat in the air fryer. Set the air fryer to 176°C for 15 minutes. Increase the temperature to 204°C for 5 minutes. Use a meat thermometer to ensure the meat has reached an internal temperature of 64°C. Let the meat rest for 10 minutes. Slice into 6 medallions and serve.

Bacon, Cheese and Pear Stuffed Pork

Prep time: 10 minutes | Cook time: 24 minutes | Serves 3

4 slices bacon, chopped
1 tablespoon butter
120 ml finely diced onion
80 ml chicken stock
355 ml seasoned stuffing mix
1 egg, beaten
½ teaspoon dried thyme
½ teaspoon salt

⅛ teaspoon black pepper
1 pear, finely diced
80 ml crumbled blue cheese
3 boneless pork chops (2-inch thick)
Olive oil
Salt and freshly ground black pepper, to taste

Preheat the air fryer to 204°C. Place the bacon into the air fryer basket and air fry for 6 minutes, stirring halfway through the cooking time. Remove the bacon and set it aside on a paper towel. Pour out the grease from the bottom of the air fryer. Make the stuffing: Melt the butter in a medium saucepan over medium heat on the stovetop. Add the onion and sauté for a few minutes, until

it starts to soften. Add the chicken stock and simmer for 1 minute. Remove the pan from the heat and add the stuffing mix. Stir until the stock has been absorbed. Add the egg, dried thyme, salt and freshly ground black pepper, and stir until combined. Fold in the diced pear and crumbled blue cheese. Place the pork chops on a cutting board. Using the palm of your hand to hold the chop flat and steady, slice into the side of the pork chop to make a pocket in the center of the chop. Leave about an inch of chop uncut and make sure you don't cut all the way through the pork chop. Brush both sides of the pork chops with olive oil and season with salt and freshly ground black pepper. Stuff each pork chop with a third of the stuffing, packing the stuffing tightly inside the pocket. Preheat the air fryer to 182°C. Spray or brush the sides of the air fryer basket with oil. Place the pork chops in the air fryer basket with the open stuffed edge of the pork chop facing the outside edges of the basket. Air fry the pork chops for 18 minutes, turning the pork chops over halfway through the cooking time. When the chops are done, let them rest for 5 minutes and then transfer to a serving platter.

Cheese Crusted Chops

Prep time: 10 minutes | Cook time: 12 minutes | Serves 4 to 6

¼ teaspoon pepper
½ teaspoons salt
4 to 6 thick boneless pork chops
235 ml pork scratching crumbs
¼ teaspoon chili powder
½ teaspoons onion granules

1 teaspoon smoked paprika
2 beaten eggs
3 tablespoons grated Parmesan cheese
Cooking spray

Preheat the air fryer to 205°C. Rub the pepper and salt on both sides of pork chops. In a food processor, pulse pork scratchings into crumbs. Mix crumbs with chili powder, onion granules, and paprika in a bowl. Beat eggs in another bowl. Dip pork chops into eggs then into pork scratchings crumb mixture. Spritz the air fryer basket with cooking spray and add pork chops to the basket. Air fry for 12 minutes. Serve garnished with the Parmesan cheese.

Smoky Pork Tenderloin

Prep time: 5 minutes | Cook time: 19 to 22 minutes | Serves 6

680 g pork tenderloin
1 tablespoon avocado oil
1 teaspoon chili powder
1 teaspoon smoked paprika

1 teaspoon garlic powder
1 teaspoon sea salt
1 teaspoon freshly ground black pepper

Pierce the tenderloin all over with a fork and rub the oil all over the meat. In a small dish, stir together the chili powder, smoked paprika, garlic powder, salt, and pepper. Rub the spice mixture all over the tenderloin. Set the air fryer to 204°C. Place the pork in the air fryer basket and air fry for 10 minutes. Flip the tenderloin and cook for 9 to 12 minutes more, until an instant-read thermometer reads at least 64°C. Allow the tenderloin to rest for 5 minutes, then slice and serve.

Bacon-Wrapped Pork Tenderloin

Prep time: 30 minutes | Cook time: 22 to 25 minutes | Serves 6

120 ml minced onion
120 ml apple cider, or apple juice
60 ml honey
1 tablespoon minced garlic
¼ teaspoon salt
¼ teaspoon freshly ground black pepper
900 g pork tenderloin
1 to 2 tablespoons oil
8 uncooked bacon slices

In a medium bowl, stir together the onion, cider, honey, garlic, salt, and pepper. Transfer to a large resealable bag or airtight container and add the pork. Seal the bag. Refrigerate to marinate for at least 2 hours. Preheat the air fryer to 204ºC. Line the air fryer basket with parchment paper. Remove the pork from the marinade and place it on the parchment. Spritz with oil. Cook for 15 minutes. Wrap the bacon slices around the pork and secure them with toothpicks. Turn the pork roast and spritz with oil. Cook for 7 to 10 minutes more until the internal temperature reaches 64ºC, depending on how well-done you like pork loin. It will continue cooking after it's removed from the fryer, so let it sit for 5 minutes before serving.

Vietnamese "Shaking" Beef

Prep time: 30 minutes | Cook time: 4 minutes per batch | Serves 4

Meat:
4 garlic cloves, minced
2 teaspoons soy sauce
2 teaspoons sugar
1 teaspoon toasted sesame oil
1 teaspoon coarse or flaky salt
¼ teaspoon black pepper
680 g flat iron or top rump steak, cut into 1-inch cubes
Salad:
2 tablespoons rice vinegar or apple cider vinegar
2 tablespoons vegetable oil
1 garlic clove, minced
2 teaspoons sugar
¼ teaspoon coarse or flaky salt
¼ teaspoon black pepper
½ red onion, halved and very thinly sliced
1 head butterhead lettuce, leaves separated and torn into large pieces
120 ml halved baby plum tomatoes
60 ml fresh mint leaves
For Serving:
Lime wedges
Coarse salt and freshly cracked black pepper, to taste

For the meat: In a small bowl, combine the garlic, soy sauce, sugar, sesame oil, salt, and pepper. Place the meat in a gallon-size resealable plastic bag. Pour the marinade over the meat. Seal and place the bag in a large bowl. Marinate for 30 minutes, or cover and refrigerate for up to 24 hours. Place half the meat in the air fryer basket. Set the air fryer to 232ºC for 4 minutes, shaking the basket to redistribute the meat halfway through the cooking time. Transfer the meat to a plate (it should be medium-rare, still pink in the middle). Cover lightly with aluminum foil. Repeat to cook the remaining meat. Meanwhile, for the salad: In a large bowl, whisk together the vinegar, vegetable oil, garlic, sugar, salt, and pepper. Add the onion. Stir to combine. Add the lettuce, tomatoes, and mint and toss to combine. Arrange the salad on a serving platter. Arrange the cooked meat over the salad. Drizzle any accumulated juices from the plate over the meat. Serve with lime wedges, coarse salt, and cracked black pepper.

Caraway Crusted Beef Steaks

Prep time: 5 minutes | Cook time: 10 minutes | Serves 4

4 beef steaks
2 teaspoons caraway seeds
2 teaspoons garlic powder
Sea salt and cayenne pepper, to taste
1 tablespoon melted butter
80 ml almond flour
2 eggs, beaten

Preheat the air fryer to 179ºC. Add the beef steaks to a large bowl and toss with the caraway seeds, garlic powder, salt and pepper until well coated. Stir together the melted butter and almond flour in a bowl. Whisk the eggs in a different bowl. Dredge the seasoned steaks in the eggs, then dip in the almond and butter mixture. Arrange the coated steaks in the air fryer basket. Air fryer for 10 minutes, or until the internal temperature of the beef steaks reaches at least 64ºC on a meat thermometer. Flip the steaks once halfway through to ensure even cooking. Transfer the steaks to plates. Let cool for 5 minutes and serve hot.

Indian Mint and Chile Kebabs

Prep time: 30 minutes | Cook time: 15 minutes | Serves 4

450 g lamb mince
120 ml finely minced onion
60 ml chopped fresh mint
60 ml chopped fresh coriander
1 tablespoon minced garlic
½ teaspoon ground turmeric
½ teaspoon cayenne pepper
¼ teaspoon ground cardamom
¼ teaspoon ground cinnamon
1 teaspoon coarse or flaky salt

In the bowl of a stand mixer fitted with the paddle attachment, combine the lamb, onion, mint, coriander, garlic, turmeric, cayenne, cardamom, cinnamon, and salt. Mix on low speed until you have a sticky mess of spiced meat. If you have time, let the mixture stand at room temperature for 30 minutes (or cover and refrigerate for up to a day or two, until you're ready to make the kebabs). Divide the meat into eight equal portions. Form each into a long sausage shape. Place the kebabs in a single layer in the air fryer basket. Set the air fryer to 176ºC for 10 minutes. Increase the air fryer temperature to 204ºC and cook for 3 to 4 minutes more to brown the kebabs. Use a meat thermometer to ensure the kebabs have reached an internal temperature of 72ºC (medium).

Herbed Beef

Prep time: 5 minutes | Cook time: 22 minutes | Serves 6

1 teaspoon dried dill
1 teaspoon dried thyme
1 teaspoon garlic powder
900 g beef steak
3 tablespoons butter

Preheat the air fryer to 182ºC. Combine the dill, thyme, and garlic powder in a small bowl, and massage into the steak. Air fry the steak in the air fryer for 20 minutes, then remove, shred, and return to the air fryer. Add the butter and air fry the shredded steak for a further 2 minutes at 185ºC. Make sure the beef is coated in the butter before serving.

Tuscan Air Fried Veal Loin

Prep time: 1 hour 10 minutes | Cook time: 12 minutes | Makes 3 veal chops

1½ teaspoons crushed fennel seeds
1 tablespoon minced fresh rosemary leaves
1 tablespoon minced garlic
1½ teaspoons lemon zest

1½ teaspoons salt
½ teaspoon red pepper flakes
2 tablespoons olive oil
3 (280 g) bone-in veal loin, about ½ inch thick

Combine all the ingredients, except for the veal loin, in a large bowl. Stir to mix well. Dunk the loin in the mixture and press to submerge. Wrap the bowl in plastic and refrigerate for at least an hour to marinate. Preheat the air fryer to 204ºC. Arrange the veal loin in the preheated air fryer and air fry for 12 minutes for medium-rare, or until it reaches your desired doneness. Serve immediately.

Pork Loin Roast

Prep time: 30 minutes | Cook time: 55 minutes | Serves 6

680 g boneless pork loin joint, washed
1 teaspoon mustard seeds
1 teaspoon garlic powder
1 teaspoon porcini powder
1 teaspoon onion granules

¾ teaspoon sea salt flakes
1 teaspoon red pepper flakes, crushed
2 dried sprigs thyme, crushed
2 tablespoons lime juice

Firstly, score the meat using a small knife; make sure to not cut too deep. In a small-sized mixing dish, combine all seasonings in the order listed above; mix to combine well. Massage the spice mix into the pork meat to evenly distribute. Drizzle with lemon juice. Set the air fryer to 182ºC. Place the pork in the air fryer basket; roast for 25 to 30 minutes. Pause the machine, check for doneness and cook for 25 minutes more.

Kheema Burgers

Prep time: 15 minutes | Cook time: 12 minutes | Serves 4

Burgers:
450 g 85% lean beef mince or lamb mince
2 large eggs, lightly beaten
1 medium brown onion, diced
60 ml chopped fresh coriander
1 tablespoon minced fresh ginger
3 cloves garlic, minced
2 teaspoons garam masala
1 teaspoon ground turmeric
½ teaspoon ground cinnamon

⅛ teaspoon ground cardamom
1 teaspoon coarse or flaky salt
1 teaspoon cayenne pepper
Raita Sauce:
235 ml grated cucumber
120 ml sour cream
¼ teaspoon coarse or flaky salt
¼ teaspoon black pepper
For Serving:
4 lettuce leaves, hamburger buns, or naan breads

For the burgers: In a large bowl, combine the beef mince, eggs, onion, coriander, ginger, garlic, garam masala, turmeric, cinnamon, cardamom, salt, and cayenne. Gently mix until ingredients are thoroughly combined. Divide the meat into four portions and form into round patties. Make a slight depression in the middle of each patty with your thumb to prevent them from puffing up into a dome shape while cooking. Place the patties in the air fryer basket. Set the air fryer to 176ºC for 12 minutes. Use a meat thermometer to ensure the burgers have reached an internal temperature of 72ºC (for medium). Meanwhile, for the sauce: In a small bowl, combine the cucumber, sour cream, salt, and pepper. To serve: Place the burgers on the lettuce, buns, or naan and top with the sauce.

Mojito Lamb Chops

Prep time: 30 minutes | Cook time: 5 minutes | Serves 2

Marinade:
2 teaspoons grated lime zest
120 ml lime juice
60 ml avocado oil
60 ml chopped fresh mint leaves
4 cloves garlic, roughly chopped
2 teaspoons fine sea salt

½ teaspoon ground black pepper
4 (1-inch-thick) lamb chops
Sprigs of fresh mint, for garnish (optional)
Lime slices, for serving (optional)

Make the marinade: Place all the ingredients for the marinade in a food processor or blender and purée until mostly smooth with a few small chunks. Transfer half of the marinade to a shallow dish and set the other half aside for serving. Add the lamb to the shallow dish, cover, and place in the refrigerator to marinate for at least 2 hours or overnight. Spray the air fryer basket with avocado oil. Preheat the air fryer to 200ºC. Remove the chops from the marinade and place them in the air fryer basket. Air fry for 5 minutes, or until the internal temperature reaches 64ºC for medium doneness. Allow the chops to rest for 10 minutes before serving with the rest of the marinade as a sauce. Garnish with fresh mint leaves and serve with lime slices, if desired. Best served fresh.

Cheese Pork Chops

Prep time: 15 minutes | Cook time: 9 to 14 minutes | Serves 4

2 large eggs
120 ml finely grated Parmesan cheese
120 ml finely ground blanched almond flour or finely crushed pork scratchings
1 teaspoon paprika

½ teaspoon dried oregano
½ teaspoon garlic powder
Salt and freshly ground black pepper, to taste
570 g (1-inch-thick) boneless pork chops
Avocado oil spray

Beat the eggs in a shallow bowl. In a separate bowl, combine the Parmesan cheese, almond flour, paprika, oregano, garlic powder, and salt and pepper to taste. Dip the pork chops into the eggs, then coat them with the Parmesan mixture, gently pressing the coating onto the meat. Spray the breaded pork chops with oil. Set the air fryer to 204ºC. Place the pork chops in the air fryer basket in a single layer, working in batches if necessary. Cook for 6 minutes. Flip the chops and spray them with more oil. Cook for another 3 to 8 minutes, until an instant-read thermometer reads 64ºC. Allow the pork chops to rest for at least 5 minutes, then serve.

Pork Shoulder with Garlicky Coriander-Parsley Sauce

Prep time: 1 hour 15 minutes | Cook time: 30 minutes | Serves 4

1 teaspoon flaxseed meal
1 egg white, well whisked
1 tablespoon soy sauce
1 teaspoon lemon juice, preferably freshly squeezed
1 tablespoon olive oil
450 g pork shoulder, cut into pieces 2-inches long
Salt and ground black pepper, to taste

Garlicky Coriander-Parsley Sauce:
3 garlic cloves, minced
80 ml fresh coriander leaves
80 ml fresh parsley leaves
1 teaspoon lemon juice
½ tablespoon salt
80 ml extra-virgin olive oil

Combine the flaxseed meal, egg white, soy sauce, lemon juice, salt, black pepper, and olive oil in a large bowl. Dunk the pork strips in and press to submerge. Wrap the bowl in plastic and refrigerate to marinate for at least an hour. Preheat the air fryer to 192°C. Arrange the marinated pork strips in the preheated air fryer and air fry for 30 minutes or until cooked through and well browned. Flip the strips halfway through. Meanwhile, combine the ingredients for the sauce in a small bowl. Stir to mix well. Arrange the bowl in the refrigerator to chill until ready to serve. Serve the air fried pork strips with the chilled sauce.

Sesame Beef Lettuce Tacos

Prep time: 30 minutes | Cook time: 8 to 10 minutes | Serves 4

60 ml soy sauce or tamari
60 ml avocado oil
2 tablespoons cooking sherry
1 tablespoon granulated sweetener
1 tablespoon ground cumin
1 teaspoon minced garlic
Sea salt and freshly ground black pepper, to taste

450 g bavette or skirt steak
8 butterhead lettuce leaves
2 spring onions, sliced
1 tablespoon toasted sesame seeds
Hot sauce, for serving
Lime wedges, for serving
Flaky sea salt (optional)

In a small bowl, whisk together the soy sauce, avocado oil, cooking sherry, sweetener, cumin, garlic, and salt and pepper to taste. Place the steak in a shallow dish. Pour the marinade over the beef. Cover the dish with plastic wrap and let it marinate in the refrigerator for at least 2 hours or overnight. Remove the flank steak from the dish and discard the marinade. Set the air fryer to 204°C. Place the steak in the air fryer basket and air fry for 4 to 6 minutes. Flip the steak and cook for 4 minutes more, until an instant-read thermometer reads 49°C at the thickest part (or cook it to your desired doneness). Allow the steak to rest for 10 minutes, then slice it thinly against the grain. Stack 2 lettuce leaves on top of each other and add some sliced meat. Top with spring onions and sesame seeds. Drizzle with hot sauce and lime juice, and finish with a little flaky salt (if using). Repeat with the remaining lettuce leaves and fillings.

Chapter 6 Vegetables and Sides

Chapter 6 Vegetables and Sides

Garlic Courgette and Red Peppers

Prep time: 5 minutes | Cook time: 15 minutes | Serves 6

2 medium courgette, cubed
1 red pepper, diced
2 garlic cloves, sliced

2 tablespoons olive oil
½ teaspoon salt

Preheat the air fryer to 193°C. In a large bowl, mix together the courgette, bell pepper, and garlic with the olive oil and salt. Pour the mixture into the air fryer basket, and roast for 7 minutes. Shake or stir, then roast for 7 to 8 minutes more.

Butternut Squash Croquettes

Prep time: 5 minutes | Cook time: 17 minutes | Serves 4

⅓ butternut squash, peeled and grated
40 g plain flour
2 eggs, whisked
4 cloves garlic, minced
1½ tablespoons olive oil

1 teaspoon fine sea salt
⅓ teaspoon freshly ground black pepper, or more to taste
⅓ teaspoon dried sage
A pinch of ground allspice

Preheat the air fryer to 170°C. Line the air fryer basket with parchment paper. In a mixing bowl, stir together all the ingredients until well combined. Make the squash croquettes: Use a small cookie scoop to drop tablespoonfuls of the squash mixture onto a lightly floured surface and shape into balls with your hands. Transfer them to the air fryer basket. Air fry for 17 minutes until the squash croquettes are golden brown. Remove from the basket to a plate and serve warm.

Parmesan Herb Focaccia Bread

Prep time: 10 minutes | Cook time: 10 minutes | Serves 6

225 g shredded Mozzarella cheese
30 g) full-fat cream cheese
95 g blanched finely ground almond flour
40 g ground golden flaxseed
20 g grated Parmesan cheese

½ teaspoon bicarbonate of soda
2 large eggs
½ teaspoon garlic powder
¼ teaspoon dried basil
¼ teaspoon dried rosemary
2 tablespoons salted butter, melted and divided

Place Mozzarella, cream cheese, and almond flour into a large microwave-safe bowl and microwave for 1 minute. Add the flaxseed, Parmesan, and bicarbonate of soda and stir until smooth ball forms. If the mixture cools too much, it will be hard to mix.

Return to microwave for 10 to 15 seconds to rewarm if necessary. Stir in eggs. You may need to use your hands to get them fully incorporated. Just keep stirring and they will absorb into the dough. Sprinkle dough with garlic powder, basil, and rosemary and knead into dough. Grease a baking pan with 1 tablespoon melted butter. Press the dough evenly into the pan. Place pan into the air fryer basket. Adjust the temperature to 200°C and bake for 10 minutes. At 7 minutes, cover with foil if bread begins to get too dark. Remove and let cool at least 30 minutes. Drizzle with remaining butter and serve.

Roasted Aubergine

Prep time: 15 minutes | Cook time: 15 minutes | Serves 4

1 large aubergine
2 tablespoons olive oil

¼ teaspoon salt
½ teaspoon garlic powder

Remove top and bottom from aubergine. Slice aubergine into ¼-inch-thick round slices. Brush slices with olive oil. Sprinkle with salt and garlic powder. Place aubergine slices into the air fryer basket. Adjust the temperature to 200°C and set the timer for 15 minutes. Serve immediately.

Garlic-Parmesan Crispy Baby Potatoes

Prep time: 10 minutes | Cook time: 15 minutes | Serves 4

Oil, for spraying
450 g baby potatoes
45 g grated Parmesan cheese, divided
3 tablespoons olive oil
2 teaspoons garlic powder
½ teaspoon onion powder

½ teaspoon salt
¼ teaspoon freshly ground black pepper
¼ teaspoon paprika
2 tablespoons chopped fresh parsley, for garnish

Line the air fryer basket with parchment and spray lightly with oil. Rinse the potatoes, pat dry with paper towels, and place in a large bowl. In a small bowl, mix together 45 g of Parmesan cheese, the olive oil, garlic, onion powder, salt, black pepper, and paprika. Pour the mixture over the potatoes and toss to coat. Transfer the potatoes to the prepared basket and spread them out in an even layer, taking care to keep them from touching. You may need to work in batches, depending on the size of your air fryer. Air fry at 200°C for 15 minutes, stirring after 7 to 8 minutes, or until easily pierced with a fork. Continue to cook for another 1 to 2 minutes, if needed. Sprinkle with the parsley and the remaining Parmesan cheese and serve.

Glazed Sweet Potato Bites

Prep time: 10 minutes | Cook time: 25 minutes | Serves 4

Oil, for spraying
3 medium sweet potatoes, peeled and cut into 1-inch pieces

2 tablespoons honey
1 tablespoon olive oil
2 teaspoons ground cinnamon

Line the air fryer basket with parchment and spray lightly with oil. In a large bowl, toss together the sweet potatoes, honey, olive oil, and cinnamon until evenly coated. Place the potatoes in the prepared basket. Air fry at 200°C for 20 to 25 minutes, or until crispy and easily pierced with a fork.

Green Tomato Salad

Prep time: 10 minutes | Cook time: 8 to 10 minutes | Serves 4

4 green tomatoes
½ teaspoon salt
1 large egg, lightly beaten
50 g peanut flour
1 tablespoon Creole seasoning
1 (140 g) bag rocket
Buttermilk Dressing:
230 g mayonnaise
120 g sour cream

2 teaspoons fresh lemon juice
2 tablespoons finely chopped fresh parsley
1 teaspoon dried dill
1 teaspoon dried chives
½ teaspoon salt
½ teaspoon garlic powder
½ teaspoon onion powder

Preheat the air fryer to 200°C. Slice the tomatoes into ½-inch slices and sprinkle with the salt. Let sit for 5 to 10 minutes. Place the egg in a small shallow bowl. In another small shallow bowl, combine the peanut flour and Creole seasoning. Dip each tomato slice into the egg wash, then dip into the peanut flour mixture, turning to coat evenly. Working in batches if necessary, arrange the tomato slices in a single layer in the air fryer basket and spray both sides lightly with olive oil. Air fry until browned and crisp, 8 to 10 minutes. To make the buttermilk dressing: In a small bowl, whisk together the mayonnaise, sour cream, lemon juice, parsley, dill, chives, salt, garlic powder, and onion powder. Serve the tomato slices on top of a bed of the rocket with the dressing on the side.

Asian-Inspired Roasted Broccoli

Prep time: 10 minutes | Cook time: 15 minutes | Serves 4

Broccoli:
Oil, for spraying
450 g broccoli florets
2 teaspoons peanut oil
1 tablespoon minced garlic
½ teaspoon salt

Sauce:
2 tablespoons soy sauce
2 teaspoons honey
2 teaspoons Sriracha
1 teaspoon rice vinegar

Make the Broccoli Line the air fryer basket with parchment and spray lightly with oil. In a large bowl, toss together the broccoli, peanut oil, garlic, and salt until evenly coated. Spread out the broccoli in an even layer in the prepared basket. Air fry at 200°C for

15 minutes, stirring halfway through. Make the Sauce Meanwhile, in a small microwave-safe bowl, combine the soy sauce, honey, Sriracha, and rice vinegar and microwave on high for about 15 seconds. Stir to combine. Transfer the broccoli to a serving bowl and add the sauce. Gently toss until evenly coated and serve immediately.

Fried Brussels Sprouts

Prep time: 10 minutes | Cook time: 18 minutes | Serves 4

1 teaspoon plus 1 tablespoon extra-virgin olive oil, divided
2 teaspoons minced garlic
2 tablespoons honey
1 tablespoon sugar
2 tablespoons freshly squeezed lemon juice
2 tablespoons rice vinegar

2 tablespoons sriracha
450 g Brussels sprouts, stems trimmed and any tough leaves removed, rinsed, halved lengthwise, and dried
½ teaspoon salt
Cooking oil spray

In a small saucepan over low heat, combine 1 teaspoon of olive oil, the garlic, honey, sugar, lemon juice, vinegar, and sriracha. Cook for 2 to 3 minutes, or until slightly thickened. Remove the pan from the heat, cover, and set aside. Place the Brussels sprouts in a resealable bag or small bowl. Add the remaining olive oil and the salt, and toss to coat. Insert the crisper plate into the basket and the basket into the unit. Preheat the unit by selecting AIR FRY, setting the temperature to 200°C, and setting the time to 3 minutes. Select START/STOP to begin. Once the unit is preheated, spray the crisper plate with cooking oil. Add the Brussels sprouts to the basket. Select AIR FRY, set the temperature to 200°C, and set the time to 15 minutes. Select START/STOP to begin. After 7 or 8 minutes, remove the basket and shake it to toss the sprouts. Reinsert the basket to resume cooking. When the cooking is complete, the leaves should be crispy and light brown and the sprout centres tender. Place the sprouts in a medium serving bowl and drizzle the sauce over the top. Toss to coat, and serve immediately.

Lemon-Garlic Mushrooms

Prep time: 10 minutes | Cook time: 10 to 15 minutes | Serves 6

340 g sliced mushrooms
1 tablespoon avocado oil
Sea salt and freshly ground black pepper, to taste
3 tablespoons unsalted butter
1 teaspoon minced garlic

1 teaspoon freshly squeezed lemon juice
½ teaspoon red pepper flakes
2 tablespoons chopped fresh parsley

Place the mushrooms in a medium bowl and toss with the oil. Season to taste with salt and pepper. Place the mushrooms in a single layer in the air fryer basket. Set your air fryer to 192°C and roast for 10 to 15 minutes, until the mushrooms are tender. While the mushrooms cook, melt the butter in a small pot or skillet over medium-low heat. Stir in the garlic and cook for 30 seconds. Remove the pot from the heat and stir in the lemon juice and red pepper flakes. Toss the mushrooms with the lemon-garlic butter and garnish with the parsley before serving.

Flatbread

Prep time: 5 minutes | Cook time: 7 minutes | Serves 2

225 g shredded Mozzarella cheese
25 g blanched finely ground

almond flour
30 g full-fat cream cheese, softened

In a large microwave-safe bowl, melt Mozzarella in the microwave for 30 seconds. Stir in almond flour until smooth and then add cream cheese. Continue mixing until dough forms, gently kneading it with wet hands if necessary. Divide the dough into two pieces and roll out to ¼-inch thickness between two pieces of parchment. Cut another piece of parchment to fit your air fryer basket. Place a piece of flatbread onto your parchment and into the air fryer, working in two batches if needed. Adjust the temperature to 160ºC and air fry for 7 minutes. Halfway through the cooking time flip the flatbread. Serve warm.

Citrus-Roasted Broccoli Florets

Prep time: 5 minutes | Cook time: 12 minutes | Serves 6

285 g broccoli florets (approximately 1 large head)
2 tablespoons olive oil
½ teaspoon salt

130 ml orange juice
1 tablespoon raw honey
Orange wedges, for serving (optional)

Preheat the air fryer to 180ºC. In a large bowl, combine the broccoli, olive oil, salt, orange juice, and honey. Toss the broccoli in the liquid until well coated. Pour the broccoli mixture into the air fryer basket and roast for 6 minutes. Stir and roast for 6 minutes more. Serve alone or with orange wedges for additional citrus flavour, if desired.

Chiles Rellenos with Red Chile Sauce

Prep time: 20 minutes | Cook time: 20 minutes | Serves 2

Peppers:
2 poblano peppers, rinsed and dried
110 g thawed frozen or drained canned corn kernels
1 spring onion, sliced
2 tablespoons chopped fresh coriander
½ teaspoon coarse sea salt
¼ teaspoon black pepper
150 g grated Monterey Jack cheese
Sauce:
3 tablespoons extra-virgin olive

oil
25 g finely chopped yellow onion
2 teaspoons minced garlic
1 (170 g) can tomato paste
2 tablespoons ancho chili powder
1 teaspoon dried oregano
1 teaspoon ground cumin
½ teaspoon coarse sea salt
470 ml chicken stock
2 tablespoons fresh lemon juice
Mexican crema or sour cream, for serving

For the peppers: Place the peppers in the air fryer basket. Set the air fryer to 200ºC for 10 minutes, turning the peppers halfway through the cooking time, until their skins are charred. Transfer the peppers to a resealable plastic bag, seal, and set aside to steam for 5 minutes. Peel the peppers and discard the skins. Cut a slit down the centre of each pepper, starting at the stem and continuing to the tip. Remove the seeds, being careful not to tear the chile. In a medium bowl, combine the corn, spring onion, coriander, salt, black pepper, and cheese; set aside. Meanwhile, for the sauce: In a large skillet, heat the olive oil over medium-high heat. Add the onion and cook, stirring, until tender, about 5 minutes. Add the garlic and cook, stirring, for 30 seconds. Stir in the tomato paste, chile powder, oregano, and cumin, and salt. Cook, stirring, for 1 minute. Whisk in the stock and lemon juice. Bring to a simmer and cook, stirring occasionally, while the stuffed peppers finish cooking. Cut a slit down the centre of each poblano pepper, starting at the stem and continuing to the tip. Remove the seeds, being careful not to tear the chile. Carefully stuff each pepper with half the corn mixture. Place the stuffed peppers in a baking pan. Place the pan in the air fryer basket. Set the air fryer to 200ºC for 10 minutes, or until the cheese has melted. Transfer the stuffed peppers to a serving platter and drizzle with the sauce and some crema.

Sweet-and-Sour Brussels Sprouts

Prep time: 10 minutes | Cook time: 20 minutes | Serves 2

70 g Thai sweet chili sauce
2 tablespoons black vinegar or balsamic vinegar
½ teaspoon hot sauce, such as Tabasco
230 g Brussels sprouts, trimmed (large sprouts halved)

2 small shallots, cut into ¼-inch-thick slices
coarse sea salt and freshly ground black pepper, to taste
2 teaspoons lightly packed fresh coriander leaves

In a large bowl, whisk together the chili sauce, vinegar, and hot sauce. Add the Brussels sprouts and shallots, season with salt and pepper, and toss to combine. Scrape the Brussels sprouts and sauce into a cake pan. Place the pan in the air fryer and roast at 192ºC, stirring every 5 minutes, until the Brussels sprouts are tender and the sauce is reduced to a sticky glaze, about 20 minutes. Remove the pan from the air fryer and transfer the Brussels sprouts to plates. Sprinkle with the coriander and serve warm.

Spinach and Sweet Pepper Poppers

Prep time: 10 minutes | Cook time: 8 minutes | Makes 16 poppers

110 g cream cheese, softened
20 g chopped fresh spinach leaves
½ teaspoon garlic powder

8 mini sweet bell peppers, tops removed, seeded, and halved lengthwise

In a medium bowl, mix cream cheese, spinach, and garlic powder. Place 1 tablespoon mixture into each sweet pepper half and press down to smooth. Place poppers into ungreased air fryer basket. Adjust the temperature to 200ºC and air fry for 8 minutes. Poppers will be done when cheese is browned on top and peppers are tender-crisp. Serve warm.

Golden Garlicky Mushrooms

Prep time: 10 minutes | Cook time: 10 minutes | Serves 4

6 small mushrooms
1 tablespoon bread crumbs
1 tablespoon olive oil
30 g onion, peeled and diced

1 teaspoon parsley
1 teaspoon garlic purée
Salt and ground black pepper, to taste

Preheat the air fryer to 180°C. Combine the bread crumbs, oil, onion, parsley, salt, pepper and garlic in a bowl. Cut out the mushrooms' stalks and stuff each cap with the crumb mixture. Air fry in the air fryer for 10 minutes. Serve hot.

Chermoula-Roasted Beetroots

Prep time: 15 minutes | Cook time: 25 minutes | Serves 4

Chermoula:
30 g packed fresh coriander leaves
15 g packed fresh parsley leaves
6 cloves garlic, peeled
2 teaspoons smoked paprika
2 teaspoons ground cumin
1 teaspoon ground coriander
½ to 1 teaspoon cayenne pepper
Pinch crushed saffron (optional)

115 ml extra-virgin olive oil
coarse sea salt, to taste
Beetroots:
3 medium beetroots, trimmed, peeled, and cut into 1-inch chunks
2 tablespoons chopped fresh coriander
2 tablespoons chopped fresh parsley

For the chermoula: In a food processor, combine the fresh coriander, parsley, garlic, paprika, cumin, ground coriander, and cayenne. Pulse until coarsely chopped. Add the saffron, if using, and process until combined. With the food processor running, slowly add the olive oil in a steady stream; process until the sauce is uniform. Season to taste with salt. For the beetroots: In a large bowl, drizzle the beetroots with ½ cup of the chermoula, or enough to coat. Arrange the beetroots in the air fryer basket. Set the air fryer to 192°C for 25 to minutes, or until the beetroots are tender. Transfer the beetroots to a serving platter. Sprinkle with chopped coriander and parsley and serve.

Parmesan-Thyme Butternut Squash

Prep time: 15 minutes | Cook time: 20 minutes | Serves 4

350 g butternut squash, cubed into 1-inch pieces (approximately 1 medium)
2 tablespoons olive oil
¼ teaspoon salt

¼ teaspoon garlic powder
¼ teaspoon black pepper
1 tablespoon fresh thyme
20 g grated Parmesan

Preheat the air fryer to 180°C. In a large bowl, combine the cubed squash with the olive oil, salt, garlic powder, pepper, and thyme until the squash is well coated. Pour this mixture into the air fryer basket, and roast for 10 minutes. Stir and roast another 8 to 10 minutes more. Remove the squash from the air fryer and toss with freshly grated Parmesan before serving.

Buffalo Cauliflower with Blue Cheese

Prep time: 15 minutes | Cook time: 5 to 7 minutes per batch | Serves 6

1 large head cauliflower, rinsed and separated into small florets
1 tablespoon extra-virgin olive oil
½ teaspoon garlic powder
Cooking oil spray
80 ml hot wing sauce

190 g nonfat Greek yogurt
60 g buttermilk
½ teaspoon hot sauce
1 celery stalk, chopped
2 tablespoons crumbled blue cheese

Insert the crisper plate into the basket and the basket into the unit. Preheat the unit by selecting AIR FRY, setting the temperature to 192°C, and setting the time to 3 minutes. Select START/STOP to begin. In a large bowl, toss together the cauliflower florets and olive oil. Sprinkle with the garlic powder and toss again to coat. Once the unit is preheated, spray the crisper plate with cooking oil. Put half the cauliflower into the basket. Select AIR FRY, set the temperature to 192°C, and set the time to 7 minutes. Select START/STOP to begin. After 3 minutes, remove the basket and shake the cauliflower. Reinsert the basket to resume cooking. After 2 minutes, check the cauliflower. It is done when it is browned. If not, resume cooking. When the cooking is complete, transfer the cauliflower to a serving bowl and toss with half the hot wing sauce. Repeat steps 4, 5, and 6 with the remaining cauliflower and hot wing sauce. In a small bowl, stir together the yogurt, buttermilk, hot sauce, celery, and blue cheese. Drizzle the sauce over the finished cauliflower and serve.

Potato with Creamy Cheese

Prep time: 5 minutes | Cook time: 15 minutes | Serves 2

2 medium potatoes
1 teaspoon butter
3 tablespoons sour cream

1 teaspoon chives
1½ tablespoons grated Parmesan cheese

Preheat the air fryer to 180°C. Pierce the potatoes with a fork and boil them in water until they are cooked. Transfer to the air fryer and air fry for 15 minutes. In the meantime, combine the sour cream, cheese and chives in a bowl. Cut the potatoes halfway to open them up and fill with the butter and sour cream mixture. Serve immediately.

Chapter 7 Snacks and Appetisers

Roasted Pearl Onion Dip

Prep time: 5 minutes | Cook time: 12 minutes | Serves 4

475 ml peeled pearl onions
3 garlic cloves
3 tablespoons olive oil, divided
½ teaspoon salt
240 ml non-fat plain Greek yoghurt

1 tablespoon lemon juice
¼ teaspoon black pepper
⅛ teaspoon red pepper flakes
Pitta chips, vegetables, or toasted bread for serving (optional)

Preheat the air fryer to 182°C. In a large bowl, combine the pearl onions and garlic with 2 tablespoons of the olive oil until the onions are well coated. Pour the garlic-and-onion mixture into the air fryer basket and roast for 12 minutes. Transfer the garlic and onions to a food processor. Pulse the vegetables several times, until the onions are minced but still have some chunks. In a large bowl, combine the garlic and onions and the remaining 1 tablespoon of olive oil, along with the salt, yoghurt, lemon juice, black pepper, and red pepper flakes. Cover and chill for 1 hour before serving with pitta chips, vegetables, or toasted bread.

Shrimp Egg Rolls

Prep time: 15 minutes | Cook time: 10 minutes per batch | Serves 4

1 tablespoon vegetable oil
½ head green or savoy cabbage, finely shredded
240 ml shredded carrots
240 ml canned bean sprouts, drained
1 tablespoon soy sauce
½ teaspoon sugar
1 teaspoon sesame oil

60 ml hoisin sauce
Freshly ground black pepper, to taste
454 g cooked shrimp, diced
60 ml spring onions
8 egg roll wrappers (or use spring roll pastry)
Vegetable oil
Duck sauce

Preheat a large sauté pan over medium-high heat. Add the oil and cook the cabbage, carrots and bean sprouts until they start to wilt, about 3 minutes. Add the soy sauce, sugar, sesame oil, hoisin sauce and black pepper. Sauté for a few more minutes. Stir in the shrimp and spring onions and cook until the vegetables are just tender. Transfer the mixture to a colander in a bowl to cool. Press or squeeze out any excess water from the filling so that you don't end up with soggy egg rolls. Make the egg rolls: Place the egg roll wrappers on a flat surface with one of the points facing towards you so they look like diamonds. Dividing the filling evenly between the eight wrappers, spoon the mixture onto the centre of the egg roll wrappers. Spread the filling across the centre of the wrappers from the left corner to the right corner but leave 2 inches from each corner empty. Brush the empty sides of the wrapper with a little water. Fold the bottom corner of the wrapper tightly up over the filling, trying to avoid making any air pockets. Fold the left corner in toward the centre and then the right corner toward the centre. It should now look like an envelope. Tightly roll the egg roll from the bottom to the top open corner. Press to seal the egg roll together, brushing with a little extra water if need be. Repeat this technique with all 8 egg rolls. Preheat the air fryer to 188°C. Spray or brush all sides of the egg rolls with vegetable oil. Air fry four egg rolls at a time for 10 minutes, turning them over halfway through the cooking time. Serve hot with duck sauce or your favourite dipping sauce.

Crispy Green Bean Fries with Lemon-Yoghurt Sauce

Prep time: 5 minutes | Cook time: 5 minutes | Serves 4

Green Beans:
1 egg
2 tablespoons water
1 tablespoon wholemeal flour
¼ teaspoon paprika
½ teaspoon garlic powder
½ teaspoon salt
60 ml wholemeal breadcrumbs

227 g whole green beans
Lemon-Yoghurt Sauce:
120 ml non-fat plain Greek yoghurt
1 tablespoon lemon juice
¼ teaspoon salt
⅛ teaspoon cayenne pepper

Make the Green Beans: Preheat the air fryer to 192°C. In a medium shallow bowl, beat together the egg and water until frothy. In a separate medium shallow bowl, whisk together the flour, paprika, garlic powder, and salt, then mix in the breadcrumbs. Spray the bottom of the air fryer with cooking spray. Dip each green bean into the egg mixture, then into the bread crumb mixture, coating the outside with the crumbs. Place the green beans in a single layer in the bottom of the air fryer basket. Fry in the air fryer for 5 minutes, or until the breading is golden brown. Make the Lemon-Yoghurt Sauce: In a small bowl, combine the yoghurt, lemon juice, salt, and cayenne. Serve the green bean fries alongside the lemon-yoghurt sauce as a snack or appetizer.

Spicy Chicken Bites

Prep time: 10 minutes | Cook time: 10 to 12 minutes | Makes 30 bites

227 g boneless and skinless chicken thighs, cut into 30 pieces

¼ teaspoon rock salt
2 tablespoons hot sauce
Cooking spray

Preheat the air fryer to 200°C. Spray the air fryer basket with cooking spray and season the chicken bites with the rock salt, then place in the basket and air fry for 10 to 12 minutes or until crispy. While the chicken bites cook, pour the hot sauce into a large bowl. Remove the bites and add to the sauce bowl, tossing to coat. Serve warm.

Turkey Burger Sliders

Prep time: 10 minutes | Cook time: 5 to 7 minutes | Makes 8 sliders

450 g minced turkey
¼ teaspoon curry powder
1 teaspoon Hoisin sauce
½ teaspoon salt
8 slider rolls

120 ml slivered red onions
120 ml slivered green or red pepper
120 ml fresh chopped pineapple
Light soft white cheese

Combine turkey, curry powder, Hoisin sauce, and salt and mix together well. Shape turkey mixture into 8 small patties. Place patties in air fryer basket and air fry at 182ºC for 5 to 7 minutes, until patties are well done, and juices run clear. Place each patty on the bottom half of a slider roll and top with onions, peppers, and pineapple. Spread the remaining bun halves with soft white cheese to taste, place on top, and serve.

Onion Pakoras

Prep time: 30 minutes | Cook time: 10 minutes per batch | Serves 2

2 medium brown or white onions, sliced (475 ml)
120 ml chopped fresh coriander
2 tablespoons vegetable oil
1 tablespoon chickpea flour
1 tablespoon rice flour, or 2

tablespoons chickpea flour
1 teaspoon ground turmeric
1 teaspoon cumin seeds
1 teaspoon rock salt
½ teaspoon cayenne pepper
Vegetable oil spray

In a large bowl, combine the onions, coriander, oil, chickpea flour, rice flour, turmeric, cumin seeds, salt, and cayenne. Stir to combine. Cover and let stand for 30 minutes or up to overnight. (This allows the onions to release moisture, creating a batter.) Mix well before using. Spray the air fryer basket generously with vegetable oil spray. Drop half of the batter in 6 heaping tablespoons into the basket. Set the air fryer to 176ºC for 8 minutes. Carefully turn the pakoras over and spray with oil spray. Set the air fryer for 2 minutes, or until the batter is cooked through and crisp. Repeat with remaining batter to make 6 more pakoras, checking at 6 minutes for doneness. Serve hot.

Pork and Cabbage Egg Rolls

Prep time: 15 minutes | Cook time: 12 minutes | Makes 12 egg rolls

Cooking oil spray
2 garlic cloves, minced
340 g minced pork
1 teaspoon sesame oil
60 ml soy sauce
2 teaspoons grated peeled fresh

ginger
475 ml shredded green cabbage
4 spring onions, green parts (white parts optional), chopped
24 egg roll wrappers

Spray a skillet with the cooking oil and place it over medium-high heat. Add the garlic and cook for 1 minute until fragrant. Add the minced pork to the skillet. Using a spoon, break the pork into smaller chunks. In a small bowl, whisk the sesame oil, soy sauce, and ginger until combined. Add the sauce to the skillet. Stir to combine and continue cooking for about 5 minutes until the pork is browned and thoroughly cooked. Stir in the cabbage and spring onions. Transfer the pork mixture to a large bowl. Lay the egg roll wrappers on a flat surface. Dip a basting brush in water and glaze each egg roll wrapper along the edges with the wet brush. This will soften the dough and make it easier to roll. Stack 2 egg roll wrappers (it works best if you double-wrap the egg rolls). Scoop 1 to 2 tablespoons of the pork mixture into the centre of each wrapper stack. Roll one long side of the wrappers up over the filling. Press firmly on the area with the filling, tucking it in lightly to secure it in place. Fold in the left and right sides. Continue rolling to close. Use the basting brush to wet the seam and seal the egg roll. Repeat with the remaining ingredients. Insert the crisper plate into the basket and the basket into the unit. Preheat the unit by selecting AIR FRY, setting the temperature to 204ºC, and setting the time to 3 minutes. Select START/STOP to begin. Once the unit is preheated, spray the crisper plate with cooking oil. Place the egg rolls into the basket. It is okay to stack them. Spray them with cooking oil. 1Select AIR FRY, set the temperature to 204ºC, and set the time to 12 minutes. Insert the basket into the unit. Select START/STOP to begin. 1After 8 minutes, use tongs to flip the egg rolls. Reinsert the basket to resume cooking. 1When the cooking is complete, serve the egg rolls hot.

Garlic-Roasted Tomatoes and Olives

Prep time: 5 minutes | Cook time: 20 minutes | Serves 6

475 ml cherry tomatoes
4 garlic cloves, roughly chopped
½ red onion, roughly chopped
240 ml black olives
240 ml green olives

1 tablespoon fresh basil, minced
1 tablespoon fresh oregano, minced
2 tablespoons olive oil
¼ to ½ teaspoon salt

Preheat the air fryer to 192ºC. In a large bowl, combine all of the ingredients and toss together so that the tomatoes and olives are coated well with the olive oil and herbs. Pour the mixture into the air fryer basket, and roast for 10 minutes. Stir the mixture well, then continue roasting for an additional 10 minutes. Remove from the air fryer, transfer to a serving bowl, and enjoy.

Veggie Salmon Nachos

Prep time: 10 minutes | Cook time: 9 to 12 minutes | Serves 6

57 g baked no-salt corn tortilla chips
1 (142 g) baked salmon fillet, flaked
120 ml canned low-salt black beans, rinsed and drained

1 red pepper, chopped
120 ml grated carrot
1 jalapeño pepper, minced
80 ml shredded low-salt low-fat Swiss cheese
1 tomato, chopped

Preheat the air fryer to 182ºC. In a baking pan, layer the tortilla chips. Top with the salmon, black beans, red pepper, carrot, jalapeño, and Swiss cheese. Bake in the air fryer for 9 to 12 minutes, or until the cheese is melted and starts to brown. Top with the tomato and serve.

Lemon Shrimp with Garlic Olive Oil

Prep time: 5 minutes | Cook time: 6 minutes | Serves 4

454 g medium shrimp, cleaned and deveined	½ teaspoon salt
60 ml plus 2 tablespoons olive oil, divided	¼ teaspoon red pepper flakes
	Lemon wedges, for serving
Juice of ½ lemon	(optional)
3 garlic cloves, minced and divided	Marinara sauce, for dipping (optional)

Preheat the air fryer to 192ºC. In a large bowl, combine the shrimp with 2 tablespoons of the olive oil, as well as the lemon juice, ⅓ of the minced garlic, salt, and red pepper flakes. Toss to coat the shrimp well. In a small ramekin, combine the remaining 60 ml of olive oil and the remaining minced garlic. Tear off a 12-by-12-inch sheet of aluminium foil. Pour the shrimp into the centre of the foil, then fold the sides up and crimp the edges so that it forms an aluminium foil bowl that is open on top. Place this packet into the air fryer basket. Roast the shrimp for 4 minutes, then open the air fryer and place the ramekin with oil and garlic in the basket beside the shrimp packet. Cook for 2 more minutes. Transfer the shrimp on a serving plate or platter with the ramekin of garlic olive oil on the side for dipping. You may also serve with lemon wedges and marinara sauce, if desired.

Mushroom Tarts

Prep time: 15 minutes | Cook time: 38 minutes | Makes 15 tarts

2 tablespoons extra-virgin olive oil, divided	60 ml dry white wine
1 small white onion, sliced	1 sheet frozen puff pastry, thawed
227 g shiitake mushrooms, sliced	240 ml shredded Gruyère cheese
¼ teaspoon sea salt	Cooking oil spray
¼ teaspoon freshly ground black pepper	1 tablespoon thinly sliced fresh chives

Insert the crisper plate into the basket and the basket into the unit. Preheat the unit by selecting BAKE, setting the temperature to 148ºC, and setting the time to 3 minutes. Select START/STOP to begin. In a heatproof bowl that fits into the basket, stir together 1 tablespoon of olive oil, the onion, and the mushrooms. Once the unit is preheated, place the bowl into the basket. Select BAKE, set the temperature to 148ºC, and set the time to 7 minutes. Select START/STOP to begin. After about 2½ minutes, stir the vegetables. Resume cooking. After another 2½ minutes, the vegetables should be browned and tender. Season with the salt and pepper and add the wine. Resume cooking until the liquid evaporates, about 2 minutes. When the cooking is complete, place the bowl on a heatproof surface. Increase the air fryer temperature to 200ºC and set the time to 3 minutes. Select START/STOP to begin. Unfold the puff pastry and cut it into 15 (3-by-3-inch) squares. Using a fork, pierce the dough and brush both sides with the remaining 1 tablespoon of olive oil. Evenly distribute half the cheese among the puff pastry squares, leaving a ½-inch border around the edges. Divide the mushroom-onion mixture among the pastry squares and

top with the remaining cheese. 1Once the unit is preheated, spray the crisper plate with cooking oil. Working in batches, place 5 tarts into the basket; do not stack or overlap. 1Select BAKE, set the temperature to 200ºC, and set the time to 8 minutes. Select START/STOP to begin. 1After 6 minutes, check the tarts; if not yet golden brown, resume cooking for about 2 minutes more. 1When the cooking is complete, remove the tarts and transfer to a wire rack to cool. Repeat steps 10, 11, and 12 with the remaining tarts. 1Serve garnished with the chives.

Italian Rice Balls

Prep time: 20 minutes | Cook time: 10 minutes | Makes 8 rice balls

355 ml cooked sticky rice	tiny pieces (small enough to stuff into olives)
½ teaspoon Italian seasoning blend	2 eggs
¾ teaspoon salt, divided	80 ml Italian breadcrumbs
8 black olives, pitted	177 ml panko breadcrumbs
28 g Mozzarella cheese, cut into	Cooking spray

Preheat air fryer to 200ºC. Stuff each black olive with a piece of Mozzarella cheese. Set aside. In a bowl, combine the cooked sticky rice, Italian seasoning blend, and ½ teaspoon of salt and stir to mix well. Form the rice mixture into a log with your hands and divide it into 8 equal portions. Mould each portion around a black olive and roll into a ball. Transfer to the freezer to chill for 10 to 15 minutes until firm. In a shallow dish, place the Italian breadcrumbs. In a separate shallow dish, whisk the eggs. In a third shallow dish, combine the panko breadcrumbs and remaining salt. One by one, roll the rice balls in the Italian breadcrumbs, then dip in the whisked eggs, finally coat them with the panko breadcrumbs. Arrange the rice balls in the air fryer basket and spritz both sides with cooking spray. Air fry for 10 minutes until the rice balls are golden brown. Flip the balls halfway through the cooking time. Serve warm.

Lemon-Pepper Chicken Drumsticks

Prep time: 30 minutes | Cook time: 30 minutes | Serves 2

2 teaspoons freshly ground coarse black pepper	4 chicken drumsticks (113 g each)
1 teaspoon baking powder	Rock salt, to taste
½ teaspoon garlic powder	1 lemon

In a small bowl, stir together the pepper, baking powder, and garlic powder. Place the drumsticks on a plate and sprinkle evenly with the baking powder mixture, turning the drumsticks so they're well coated. Let the drumsticks stand in the refrigerator for at least 1 hour or up to overnight. Sprinkle the drumsticks with salt, then transfer them to the air fryer, standing them bone-end up and leaning against the wall of the air fryer basket. Air fry at 192ºC until cooked through and crisp on the outside, about 30 minutes. Transfer the drumsticks to a serving platter and finely grate the zest of the lemon over them while they're hot. Cut the lemon into wedges and serve with the warm drumsticks.

Hush Puppies

Prep time: 45 minutes | Cook time: 10 minutes | Serves 12

240 ml self-raising yellow cornmeal	1 large egg
120 ml plain flour	80 ml canned creamed corn
1 teaspoon sugar	240 ml minced onion
1 teaspoon salt	2 teaspoons minced jalapeño pepper
1 teaspoon freshly ground black pepper	2 tablespoons olive oil, divided

Thoroughly combine the cornmeal, flour, sugar, salt, and pepper in a large bowl. Whisk together the egg and corn in a small bowl. Pour the egg mixture into the bowl of cornmeal mixture and stir to combine. Stir in the minced onion and jalapeño. Cover the bowl with plastic wrap and place in the refrigerator for 30 minutes. Preheat the air fryer to 192ºC. Line the air fryer basket with parchment paper and lightly brush it with 1 tablespoon of olive oil. Scoop out the cornmeal mixture and form into 24 balls, about 1 inch. Arrange the balls in the parchment paper-lined basket, leaving space between each ball. Air fry in batches for 5 minutes. Shake the basket and brush the balls with the remaining 1 tablespoon of olive oil. Continue cooking for 5 minutes until golden brown. Remove the balls (hush puppies) from the basket and serve on a plate.

Ranch Oyster Snack Crackers

Prep time: 3 minutes | Cook time: 12 minutes | Serves 6

Oil, for spraying	½ teaspoon granulated garlic
60 ml olive oil	½ teaspoon salt
2 teaspoons dry ranch seasoning	1 (255 g) bag oyster crackers or low-salt crackers
1 teaspoon chilli powder	
½ teaspoon dried dill	

Preheat the air fryer to 164ºC. Line the air fryer basket with parchment and spray lightly with oil. In a large bowl, mix together the olive oil, ranch seasoning, chilli powder, dill, garlic, and salt. Add the crackers and toss until evenly coated. Place the mixture in the prepared basket. Cook for 10 to 12 minutes, shaking or stirring every 3 to 4 minutes, or until crisp and golden brown.

Authentic Scotch Eggs

Prep time: 15 minutes | Cook time: 11 to 13 minutes | Serves 6

680 g bulk lean chicken or turkey sausage	divided
3 raw eggs, divided	120 ml plain flour
355 ml dried breadcrumbs,	6 hardboiled eggs, peeled
	Cooking oil spray

In a large bowl, combine the chicken sausage, 1 raw egg, and 120 ml of breadcrumbs and mix well. Divide the mixture into 6 pieces and flatten each into a long oval. In a shallow bowl, beat the remaining 2 raw eggs. Place the flour in a small bowl. Place the remaining 240 ml of breadcrumbs in a second small bowl.

Roll each hardboiled egg in the flour and wrap one of the chicken sausage pieces around each egg to encircle it completely. One at a time, roll the encased eggs in the flour, dip in the beaten eggs, and finally dip in the breadcrumbs to coat. Insert the crisper plate into the basket and the basket into the unit. Preheat the unit by selecting AIR FRY, setting the temperature to 192ºC, and setting the time to 3 minutes. Select START/STOP to begin. Once the unit is preheated, spray the crisper plate with cooking oil. Place the eggs in a single layer into the basket and spray them with oil. Select AIR FRY, set the temperature to 192ºC, and set the time to 13 minutes. Select START/STOP to begin. 1After about 6 minutes, use tongs to turn the eggs and spray them with more oil. Resume cooking for 5 to 7 minutes more, or until the chicken is thoroughly cooked and the Scotch eggs are browned. 1When the cooking is complete, serve warm.

Lemony Pear Chips

Prep time: 15 minutes | Cook time: 9 to 13 minutes | Serves 4

2 firm Bosc or Anjou pears, cut crosswise into ⅛-inch-thick slices	lemon juice
	½ teaspoon ground cinnamon
1 tablespoon freshly squeezed	⅛ teaspoon ground cardamom

Preheat the air fryer to 192ºC. Separate the smaller stem-end pear rounds from the larger rounds with seeds. Remove the core and seeds from the larger slices. Sprinkle all slices with lemon juice, cinnamon, and cardamom. Put the smaller chips into the air fryer basket. Air fry for 3 to 5 minutes, or until light golden brown, shaking the basket once during cooking. Remove from the air fryer. Repeat with the larger slices, air frying for 6 to 8 minutes, or until light golden brown, shaking the basket once during cooking. Remove the chips from the air fryer. Cool and serve or store in an airtight container at room temperature up for to 2 days.

Tangy Fried Pickle Spears

Prep time: 5 minutes | Cook time: 15 minutes | Serves 6

2 jars sweet and sour pickle spears, patted dry	1 teaspoon sea salt
	½ teaspoon shallot powder
2 medium-sized eggs	⅓ teaspoon chilli powder
80 ml milk	80 ml plain flour
1 teaspoon garlic powder	Cooking spray

Preheat the air fryer to 196ºC. Spritz the air fryer basket with cooking spray. In a bowl, beat together the eggs with milk. In another bowl, combine garlic powder, sea salt, shallot powder, chilli powder and plain flour until well blended. One by one, roll the pickle spears in the powder mixture, then dredge them in the egg mixture. Dip them in the powder mixture a second time for additional coating. Arrange the coated pickles in the prepared basket. Air fry for 15 minutes until golden and crispy, shaking the basket halfway through to ensure even cooking. Transfer to a plate and let cool for 5 minutes before serving.

Carrot Chips

Prep time: 15 minutes | Cook time: 8 to 10 minutes | Serves 4

1 tablespoon olive oil, plus more for greasing the basket
4 to 5 medium carrots, trimmed and thinly sliced
1 teaspoon seasoned salt

Preheat the air fryer to 200°C. Grease the air fryer basket with the olive oil. Toss the carrot slices with 1 tablespoon of olive oil and salt in a medium bowl until thoroughly coated. Arrange the carrot slices in the greased basket. You may need to work in batches to avoid overcrowding. Air fry for 8 to 10 minutes until the carrot slices are crisp-tender. Shake the basket once during cooking. Transfer the carrot slices to a bowl and repeat with the remaining carrots. Allow to cool for 5 minutes and serve.

Easy Spiced Nuts

Prep time: 5 minutes | Cook time: 25 minutes | Makes 3 L

1 egg white, lightly beaten
60 ml sugar
1 teaspoon salt
½ teaspoon ground cinnamon
¼ teaspoon ground cloves
¼ teaspoon ground allspice
Pinch ground cayenne pepper
240 ml pecan halves
240 ml cashews
240 ml almonds

Combine the egg white with the sugar and spices in a bowl. Preheat the air fryer to 148°C. Spray or brush the air fryer basket with vegetable oil. Toss the nuts together in the spiced egg white and transfer the nuts to the air fryer basket. Air fry for 25 minutes, stirring the nuts in the basket a few times during the cooking process. Taste the nuts (carefully because they will be very hot) to see if they are crunchy and nicely toasted. Air fry for a few more minutes if necessary. Serve warm or cool to room temperature and store in an airtight container for up to two weeks.

Spinach and Crab Meat Cups

Prep time: 10 minutes | Cook time: 10 minutes | Makes 30 cups

1 (170 g) can crab meat, drained to yield 80 ml meat
60 ml frozen spinach, thawed, drained, and chopped
1 clove garlic, minced
120 ml grated Parmesan cheese
3 tablespoons plain yoghurt
¼ teaspoon lemon juice
½ teaspoon Worcestershire sauce
30 mini frozen filo shells, thawed
Cooking spray

Preheat the air fryer to 200°C. Remove any bits of shell that might remain in the crab meat. Mix the crab meat, spinach, garlic, and cheese together. Stir in the yoghurt, lemon juice, and Worcestershire sauce and mix well. Spoon a teaspoon of filling into each filo shell. Spray the air fryer basket with cooking spray and arrange half the shells in the basket. Air fry for 5 minutes. Repeat with the remaining shells. Serve immediately.

Bruschetta with Basil Pesto

Prep time: 10 minutes | Cook time: 5 to 11 minutes | Serves 4

8 slices French bread, ½ inch thick
2 tablespoons softened butter
240 ml shredded Mozzarella cheese
120 ml basil pesto
240 ml chopped grape tomatoes
2 spring onions, thinly sliced

Preheat the air fryer to 176°C. Spread the bread with the butter and place butter-side up in the air fryer basket. Bake for 3 to 5 minutes, or until the bread is light golden brown. Remove the bread from the basket and top each piece with some of the cheese. Return to the basket in 2 batches and bake for 1 to 3 minutes, or until the cheese melts. Meanwhile, combine the pesto, tomatoes, and spring onions in a small bowl. When the cheese has melted, remove the bread from the air fryer and place on a serving plate. Top each slice with some of the pesto mixture and serve.

Cheesy Steak Fries

Prep time: 5 minutes | Cook time: 20 minutes | Serves 5

1 (794 g) bag frozen steak fries
Cooking spray
Salt and pepper, to taste
120 ml beef gravy
240 ml shredded Mozzarella cheese
2 spring onions, green parts only, chopped

Preheat the air fryer to 204°C. Place the frozen steak fries in the air fryer. Air fry for 10 minutes. Shake the basket and spritz the fries with cooking spray. Sprinkle with salt and pepper. Air fry for an additional 8 minutes. Pour the beef gravy into a medium, microwave-safe bowl. Microwave for 30 seconds, or until the gravy is warm. Sprinkle the fries with the cheese. Air fry for an additional 2 minutes, until the cheese is melted. Transfer the fries to a serving dish. Drizzle the fries with gravy and sprinkle the spring onions on top for a green garnish. Serve.

Browned Ricotta with Capers and Lemon

Prep time: 10 minutes | Cook time: 8 to 10 minutes | Serves 4 to 6

355 ml whole milk ricotta cheese
2 tablespoons extra-virgin olive oil
2 tablespoons capers, rinsed
Zest of 1 lemon, plus more for garnish
1 teaspoon finely chopped fresh rosemary
Pinch crushed red pepper flakes
Salt and freshly ground black pepper, to taste
1 tablespoon grated Parmesan cheese

Preheat the air fryer to 192°C. In a mixing bowl, stir together the ricotta cheese, olive oil, capers, lemon zest, rosemary, red pepper flakes, salt, and pepper until well combined. Spread the mixture evenly in a baking dish and place it in the air fryer basket. Air fry for 8 to 10 minutes until the top is nicely browned. Remove from the basket and top with a sprinkle of grated Parmesan cheese. Garnish with the lemon zest and serve warm.

Spiced Roasted Cashews

Prep time: 5 minutes | Cook time: 10 minutes | Serves 4

475 ml raw cashews
2 tablespoons olive oil
¼ teaspoon salt

¼ teaspoon chilli powder
⅛ teaspoon garlic powder
⅛ teaspoon smoked paprika

Preheat the air fryer to 182°C. In a large bowl, toss all of the ingredients together. Pour the cashews into the air fryer basket and roast them for 5 minutes. Shake the basket, then cook for 5 minutes more. Serve immediately.

Dark Chocolate and Cranberry Granola Bars

Prep time: 5 minutes | Cook time: 15 minutes | Serves 6

475 ml certified gluten-free quick oats
2 tablespoons sugar-free dark chocolate chunks
2 tablespoons unsweetened dried cranberries

3 tablespoons unsweetened shredded coconut
120 ml raw honey
1 teaspoon ground cinnamon
⅛ teaspoon salt
2 tablespoons olive oil

Preheat the air fryer to 182°C. Line an 8-by-8-inch baking dish with parchment paper that comes up the side so you can lift it out after cooking. In a large bowl, mix together all of the ingredients until well combined. Press the oat mixture into the pan in an even layer. Place the pan into the air fryer basket and bake for 15 minutes. Remove the pan from the air fryer and lift the granola cake out of the pan using the edges of the parchment paper. Allow to cool for 5 minutes before slicing into 6 equal bars. Serve immediately or wrap in plastic wrap and store at room temperature for up to 1 week.

Mexican Potato Skins

Prep time: 10 minutes | Cook time: 55 minutes | Serves 6

Olive oil
6 medium russet or Maris Piper potatoes, scrubbed
Salt and freshly ground black pepper, to taste
240 ml fat-free refried black

beans
1 tablespoon taco seasoning
120 ml salsa
177 ml low-fat shredded Cheddar cheese

Spray the air fryer basket lightly with olive oil. Spray the potatoes lightly with oil and season with salt and pepper. Pierce each potato a few times with a fork. Place the potatoes in the air fryer basket. Air fry at 204°C until fork-tender, 30 to 40 minutes. The cooking time will depend on the size of the potatoes. You can cook the potatoes in the microwave or a standard oven, but they won't get the same lovely crispy skin they will get in the air fryer. While the potatoes are cooking, in a small bowl, mix together the beans and taco seasoning. Set aside until the potatoes are cool enough to handle. Cut each potato in half lengthwise. Scoop out most of the insides, leaving about ¼ inch in the skins so the potato skins hold their shape. Season the insides of the potato skins with salt

and black pepper. Lightly spray the insides of the potato skins with oil. You may need to cook them in batches. Place them into the air fryer basket, skin-side down, and air fry until crisp and golden, 8 to 10 minutes. Transfer the skins to a work surface and spoon ½ tablespoon of seasoned refried black beans into each one. Top each with 2 teaspoons salsa and 1 tablespoon shredded Cheddar cheese. Place filled potato skins in the air fryer basket in a single layer. Lightly spray with oil. 1Air fry until the cheese is melted and bubbly, 2 to 3 minutes.

Shrimp Toasts with Sesame Seeds

Prep time: 15 minutes | Cook time: 6 to 8 minutes | Serves 4 to 6

230 g raw shrimp, peeled and deveined
1 egg, beaten
2 spring onions, chopped, plus more for garnish
2 tablespoons chopped fresh coriander
2 teaspoons grated fresh ginger

1 to 2 teaspoons sriracha sauce
1 teaspoon soy sauce
½ teaspoon toasted sesame oil
6 slices thinly sliced white sandwich bread
120 ml sesame seeds
Cooking spray
Thai chilli sauce, for serving

Preheat the air fryer to 204°C. Spritz the air fryer basket with cooking spray. In a food processor, add the shrimp, egg, spring onions, coriander, ginger, sriracha sauce, soy sauce and sesame oil, and pulse until chopped finely. You'll need to stop the food processor occasionally to scrape down the sides. Transfer the shrimp mixture to a bowl. On a clean work surface, cut the crusts off the sandwich bread. Using a brush, generously brush one side of each slice of bread with shrimp mixture. Place the sesame seeds on a plate. Press bread slices, shrimp-side down, into sesame seeds to coat evenly. Cut each slice diagonally into quarters. Spread the coated slices in a single layer in the air fryer basket. Air fry in batches for 6 to 8 minutes, or until golden and crispy. Flip the bread slices halfway through. Repeat with the remaining bread slices. Transfer to a plate and let cool for 5 minutes. Top with the chopped spring onions and serve warm with Thai chilli sauce.

Air Fried Pot Stickers

Prep time: 10 minutes | Cook time: 18 to 20 minutes | Makes 30 pot stickers

120 ml finely chopped cabbage
60 ml finely chopped red pepper
2 spring onions, finely chopped
1 egg, beaten
2 tablespoons cocktail sauce

2 teaspoons low-salt soy sauce
30 wonton wrappers
1 tablespoon water, for brushing the wrappers

Preheat the air fryer to 182°C. In a small bowl, combine the cabbage, pepper, spring onions, egg, cocktail sauce, and soy sauce, and mix well. Put about 1 teaspoon of the mixture in the centre of each wonton wrapper. Fold the wrapper in half, covering the filling; dampen the edges with water, and seal. You can crimp the edges of the wrapper with your fingers, so they look like the pot stickers you get in restaurants. Brush them with water. Place the pot stickers in the air fryer basket and air fry in 2 batches for 9 to 10 minutes, or until the pot stickers are hot and the bottoms are lightly browned. Serve hot.

Rumaki

283 g raw chicken livers

1 can sliced water chestnuts, drained

60 ml low-salt teriyaki sauce

12 slices turkey bacon

Cut livers into 1½-inch pieces, trimming out tough veins as you slice. Place livers, water chestnuts, and teriyaki sauce in small container with lid. If needed, add another tablespoon of teriyaki sauce to make sure livers are covered. Refrigerate for 1 hour. When ready to cook, cut bacon slices in half crosswise. Wrap 1 piece of liver and 1 slice of water chestnut in each bacon strip. Secure with toothpick. When you have wrapped half of the livers, place them in the air fryer basket in a single layer. Air fry at 200°C for 10 to 12 minutes, until liver is done, and bacon is crispy. While first batch cooks, wrap the remaining livers. Repeat step 6 to cook your second batch.

Chapter 8 Desserts

Chapter 8 Desserts

Berry Crumble

Prep time: 10 minutes | Cook time: 15 minutes | Serves 4

For the Filling:
300 g mixed berries
2 tablespoons sugar
1 tablespoon cornflour
1 tablespoon fresh lemon juice
For the Topping:
30 g plain flour
20 g rolled oats
1 tablespoon granulated sugar
2 tablespoons cold unsalted butter, cut into small cubes
Whipped cream or ice cream (optional)

Preheat the air fryer to 204°C. For the filling: In a round baking pan, gently mix the berries, sugar, cornflour, and lemon juice until thoroughly combined. For the topping: In a small bowl, combine the flour, oats, and sugar. Stir the butter into the flour mixture until the mixture has the consistency of breadcrumbs. Sprinkle the topping over the berries. Put the pan in the air fryer basket and air fry for 15 minutes. Let cool for 5 minutes on a wire rack. Serve topped with whipped cream or ice cream, if desired.

Pecan Brownies

Prep time: 10 minutes | Cook time: 20 minutes | Serves 6

50 g blanched finely ground almond flour
55 g powdered sweetener
2 tablespoons unsweetened cocoa powder
½ teaspoon baking powder
55 g unsalted butter, softened
1 large egg
35 g chopped pecans
40 g low-carb, sugar-free chocolate chips

In a large bowl, mix almond flour, sweetener, cocoa powder, and baking powder. Stir in butter and egg. Fold in pecans and chocolate chips. Scoop mixture into a round baking pan. Place pan into the air fryer basket. Adjust the temperature to 148°C and bake for 20 minutes. When fully cooked a toothpick inserted in center will come out clean. Allow 20 minutes to fully cool and firm up.

Baked Brazilian Pineapple

Prep time: 10 minutes | Cook time: 10 minutes | Serves 4

95 g brown sugar
2 teaspoons ground cinnamon
1 small pineapple, peeled,
cored, and cut into spears
3 tablespoons unsalted butter, melted

In a small bowl, mix the brown sugar and cinnamon until thoroughly combined. Brush the pineapple spears with the melted butter. Sprinkle the cinnamon-sugar over the spears, pressing lightly to ensure it adheres well. Place the spears in the air fryer basket in a single layer. (Depending on the size of your air fryer, you may have to do this in batches.) Set the air fryer to 204°C and cook for 10 minutes for the first batch (6 to 8 minutes for the next batch, as the fryer will be preheated). Halfway through the cooking time, brush the spears with butter. The pineapple spears are done when they are heated through, and the sugar is bubbling. Serve hot.

Vanilla and Cardamon Walnuts Tart

Prep time: 5 minutes | Cook time: 13 minutes | Serves 6

240 ml coconut milk
60 g walnuts, ground
60 g powdered sweetener
55 g almond flour
55 g butter, at room temperature
2 eggs
1 teaspoon vanilla essence
¼ teaspoon ground cardamom
¼ teaspoon ground cloves
Cooking spray

Preheat the air fryer to 184°C. Coat a baking pan with cooking spray. Combine all the ingredients except the oil in a large bowl and stir until well blended. Spoon the batter mixture into the baking pan. Bake in the preheated air fryer for approximately 13 minutes. Check the tart for doneness: If a toothpick inserted into the center of the tart comes out clean, it's done. Remove from the air fryer and place on a wire rack to cool. Serve immediately.

Pears with Honey-Lemon Ricotta

Prep time: 10 minutes | Cook time: 8 minutes | Serves 4

2 large Bartlett pears
3 tablespoons butter, melted
3 tablespoons brown sugar
½ teaspoon ground ginger
¼ teaspoon ground cardamom
125 g full-fat ricotta cheese
1 tablespoon honey, plus additional for drizzling
1 teaspoon pure almond extract
1 teaspoon pure lemon extract

Peel each pear and cut in half, lengthwise. Use a melon baller to scoop out the core. Place the pear halves in a medium bowl, add the melted butter, and toss. Add the brown sugar, ginger, and cardamom; toss to coat. Place the pear halves, cut side down, in the air fryer basket. Set the air fryer to 192°C cooking for 8 to 10 minutes, or until the pears are lightly browned and tender, but not mushy. Meanwhile, in a medium bowl, combine the ricotta, honey, and almond and lemon extracts. Beat with an electric mixer on medium speed until the mixture is light and fluffy, about 1 minute. To serve, divide the ricotta mixture among four small shallow bowls. Place a pear half, cut side up, on top of the cheese. Drizzle with additional honey and serve.

Pretzels

Prep time: 10 minutes | Cook time: 10 minutes | Serves 6

335 g shredded Mozzarella cheese	2 tablespoons salted butter, melted, divided
110 g blanched finely ground almond flour	50 g granular sweetener, divided
	1 teaspoon ground cinnamon

Place Mozzarella, flour, 1 tablespoon butter, and 2 tablespoons sweetener in a large microwave-safe bowl. Microwave on high 45 seconds, then stir with a fork until a smooth dough ball forms. Separate dough into six equal sections. Gently roll each section into a 12-inch rope, then fold into a pretzel shape. Place pretzels into ungreased air fryer basket. Adjust the temperature to 188ºC and set the timer for 8 minutes, turning pretzels halfway through cooking. In a small bowl, combine remaining butter, remaining sweetener, and cinnamon. Brush ½ mixture on both sides of pretzels. Place pretzels back into air fryer and cook an additional 2 minutes. Transfer pretzels to a large plate. Brush on both sides with remaining butter mixture, then let cool 5 minutes before serving.

Hazelnut Butter Cookies

Prep time: 30 minutes | Cook time: 20 minutes | Serves 10

4 tablespoons liquid monk fruit, or agave syrup	190 g almond flour
65 g hazelnuts, ground	110 g coconut flour
110 g unsalted butter, room temperature	55 g granulated sweetener
	2 teaspoons ground cinnamon

Firstly, cream liquid monk fruit with butter until the mixture becomes fluffy. Sift in both types of flour. Now, stir in the hazelnuts. Now, knead the mixture to form a dough; place in the refrigerator for about 35 minutes. To finish, shape the prepared dough into the bite-sized balls; arrange them on a baking dish; flatten the balls using the back of a spoon. Mix granulated sweetener with ground cinnamon. Press your cookies in the cinnamon mixture until they are completely covered. Bake the cookies for 20 minutes at 154ºC. Leave them to cool for about 10 minutes before transferring them to a wire rack. Bon appétit!

Mixed Berry Hand Pies

Prep time: 5 minutes | Cook time: 30 minutes | Serves 4

150 g granulated sugar	two equal portions
½ teaspoon ground cinnamon	1 teaspoon water
1 tablespoon cornflour	1 package refrigerated shortcrust pastry (or your own homemade pastry)
150 g blueberries	
150 g blackberries	
150 g raspberries, divided into	1 egg, beaten

Combine the sugar, cinnamon, and cornstarch in a small saucepan. Add the blueberries, blackberries, and ½ of the raspberries. Toss the berries gently to coat them evenly. Add the teaspoon of water to the saucepan and turn the stovetop on to medium-high heat, stirring occasionally. Once the berries break down, release their juice, and start to simmer (about 5 minutes), simmer for another couple of minutes and then transfer the mixture to a bowl, stir in the remaining ½ of the raspberries and let it cool. Preheat the air fryer to 188ºC. Cut the pie dough into four 5-inch circles and four 6-inch circles. Spread the 6-inch circles on a flat surface. Divide the berry filling between all four circles. Brush the perimeter of the dough circles with a little water. Place the 5-inch circles on top of the filling and press the perimeter of the dough circles together to seal. Roll the edges of the bottom circle up over the top circle to make a crust around the filling. Press a fork around the crust to make decorative indentations and to seal the crust shut. Brush the pies with egg wash and sprinkle a little sugar on top. Poke a small hole in the center of each pie with a paring knife to vent the dough. Air fry two pies at a time. Brush or spray the air fryer basket with oil and place the pies into the basket. Air fry for 9 minutes. Turn the pies over and air fry for another 6 minutes. Serve warm or at room temperature.

Pecan Bars

Prep time: 5 minutes | Cook time: 40 minutes | Serves 12

220 g coconut flour	softened
5 tablespoons granulated sweetener	60 ml heavy cream
	1 egg, beaten
4 tablespoons coconut oil,	4 pecans, chopped

Mix coconut flour, sweetener, coconut oil, heavy cream, and egg. Pour the batter in the air fryer basket and flatten well. Top the mixture with pecans and cook the meal at 176ºC for 40 minutes. Cut the cooked meal into the bars.

Lush Chocolate Chip Cookies

Prep time: 7 minutes | Cook time: 9 minutes | Serves 4

3 tablespoons butter, at room temperature	chocolate
	¼ teaspoon baking soda
65 g light brown sugar, plus 1 tablespoon	½ teaspoon vanilla extract
1 egg yolk	120 g semisweet chocolate chips
70 g plain flour	Nonstick flour-infused baking spray
2 tablespoons ground white	

In medium bowl, beat together the butter and brown sugar until fluffy. Stir in the egg yolk. Add the flour, white chocolate, baking soda, and vanilla and mix well. Stir in the chocolate chips. Line a 6-by-2-inch round baking pan with baking paper. Spray the baking paper with flour-infused baking spray. Insert the crisper plate into the basket and the basket into the unit. Preheat the unit to 148ºC. Spread the batter into the prepared pan, leaving a ½-inch border on all sides. Once the unit is preheated, place the pan into the basket. Bake to cookies for 9 minutes. When the cooking is complete, the cookies should be light brown and just barely set. Remove the pan from the basket and let cool for 10 minutes. Remove the cookie from the pan, remove the baking paper, and let cool completely on a wire rack.

Funnel Cake

Prep time: 10 minutes | Cook time: 5 minutes | Serves 4

Coconut, or avocado oil, for spraying
110 g self-raising flour, plus more for dusting
240 ml fat-free vanilla Greek yogurt
½ teaspoon ground cinnamon
¼ cup icing sugar

Preheat the air fryer to 192°C. Line the air fryer basket with baking paper, and spray lightly with oil. In a large bowl, mix together the flour, yogurt and cinnamon until the mixture forms a ball. Place the dough on a lightly floured work surface and knead for about 2 minutes. Cut the dough into 4 equal pieces, then cut each of those into 6 pieces. You should have 24 pieces in total. Roll the pieces into 8- to 10-inch-long ropes. Loosely mound the ropes into 4 piles of 6 ropes. Place the dough piles in the prepared basket, and spray liberally with oil. You may need to work in batches, depending on the size of your air fryer. Cook for 5 minutes, or until lightly browned. Dust with the icing sugar before serving.

Pecan and Cherry Stuffed Apples

Prep time: 10 minutes | Cook time: 20 minutes | Serves 4

4 apples (about 565 g)
40 g chopped pecans
50 g dried tart cherries
1 tablespoon melted butter
3 tablespoons brown sugar
¼ teaspoon allspice
Pinch salt
Ice cream, for serving

Cut off top ½ inch from each apple; reserve tops. With a melon baller, core through stem ends without breaking through the bottom. (Do not trim bases.) Preheat the air fryer to 176°C. Combine pecans, cherries, butter, brown sugar, allspice, and a pinch of salt. Stuff mixture into the hollow centers of the apples. Cover with apple tops. Put in the air fryer basket, using tongs. Air fry for 20 to 25 minutes, or just until tender. Serve warm with ice cream.

Chocolate Peppermint Cheesecake

Prep time: 5 minutes | Cook time: 18 minutes | Serves 6

Crust:
110 g butter, melted
55 g coconut flour
2 tablespoons granulated sweetener
Cooking spray
Topping:
110 g unsweetened cooking chocolate
180 g mascarpone cheese, at room temperature
1 teaspoon vanilla extract
2 drops peppermint extract

Preheat the air fryer to 176°C. Lightly coat a baking pan with cooking spray. In a mixing bowl, whisk together the butter, flour, and sweetener until well combined. Transfer the mixture to the prepared baking pan. Place the baking pan in the air fryer and bake for 18 minutes until a toothpick inserted in the center comes out clean. Remove the crust from the air fryer to a wire rack to cool. Once cooled completely, place it in the freezer for 20 minutes.

When ready, combine all the ingredients for the topping in a small bowl and stir to incorporate. Spread this topping over the crust and let it sit for another 15 minutes in the freezer. Serve chilled.

Crumbly Coconut-Pecan Cookies

Prep time: 10 minutes | Cook time: 25 minutes | Serves 10

170 g coconut flour
170 g extra-fine almond flour
½ teaspoon baking powder
⅓ teaspoon baking soda
3 eggs plus an egg yolk, beaten
175 ml coconut oil, at room temperature
125 g unsalted pecan nuts, roughly chopped
150 g monk fruit, or equivalent sweetener
¼ teaspoon freshly grated nutmeg
⅓ teaspoon ground cloves
½ teaspoon pure vanilla extract
½ teaspoon pure coconut extract
⅛ teaspoon fine sea salt

Preheat the air fryer to 188°C. Line the air fryer basket with baking paper. Mix the coconut flour, almond flour, baking powder, and baking soda in a large mixing bowl. In another mixing bowl, stir together the eggs and coconut oil. Add the wet mixture to the dry mixture. Mix in the remaining ingredients and stir until a soft dough forms. Drop about 2 tablespoons of dough on the baking paper for each cookie and flatten each biscuit until it's 1 inch thick. Bake for about 25 minutes until the cookies are golden and firm to the touch. Remove from the basket to a plate. Let the cookies cool to room temperature and serve.

Pineapple Wontons

Prep time: 15 minutes | Cook time: 15 to 18 minutes per batch | Serves 5

225 g cream cheese
170 g finely chopped fresh pineapple
20 wonton wrappers
Cooking oil spray

In a small microwave-safe bowl, heat the cream cheese in the microwave on high power for 20 seconds to soften. In a medium bowl, stir together the cream cheese and pineapple until mixed well. Lay out the wonton wrappers on a work surface. A clean table or large cutting board works well. Spoon 1½ teaspoons of the cream cheese mixture onto each wrapper. Be careful not to overfill. Fold each wrapper diagonally across to form a triangle. Bring the 2 bottom corners up toward each other. Do not close the wrapper yet. Bring up the 2 open sides and push out any air. Squeeze the open edges together to seal. Insert the crisper plate into the basket and the basket into the unit. Preheat the air fryer to 200°C. Once the unit is preheated, spray the crisper plate with cooking oil. Place the wontons into the basket. You can work in batches or stack the wontons. Spray the wontons with the cooking oil. Cook wontons for 10 minutes, then remove the basket, flip each wonton, and spray them with more oil. Reinsert the basket to resume cooking for 5 to 8 minutes more until the wontons are light golden brown and crisp. If cooking in batches, remove the cooked wontons from the basket and repeat steps 7 and 8 for the remaining wontons. 1When the cooking is complete, cool for 5 minutes before serving.

Gluten-Free Spice Cookies

Prep time: 10 minutes | Cook time: 12 minutes | Serves 4

4 tablespoons unsalted butter, at room temperature	2 teaspoons ground ginger
2 tablespoons agave nectar	1 teaspoon ground cinnamon
1 large egg	½ teaspoon freshly grated nutmeg
2 tablespoons water	1 teaspoon baking soda
240 g almond flour	¼ teaspoon kosher, or coarse sea salt
100 g granulated sugar	

Line the bottom of the air fryer basket with baking paper cut to fit. In a large bowl, using a hand mixer, beat together the butter, agave, egg, and water on medium speed until light and fluffy. Add the almond flour, sugar, ginger, cinnamon, nutmeg, baking soda, and salt. Beat on low speed until well combined. Roll the dough into 2-tablespoon balls and arrange them on the baking paper in the basket. (They don't really spread too much but try to leave a little room between them.) Set the air fryer to 164°C, and cook for 12 minutes, or until the tops of cookies are lightly browned. Transfer to a wire rack and let cool completely. Store in an airtight container for up to a week.

Chocolate Croissants

Prep time: 5 minutes | Cook time: 24 minutes | Serves 8

1 sheet frozen puff pastry, thawed	100 g chocolate-hazelnut spread
	1 large egg, beaten

On a lightly floured surface, roll puff pastry into a 14-inch square. Cut pastry into quarters to form 4 squares. Cut each square diagonally to form 8 triangles. Spread 2 teaspoons chocolate-hazelnut spread on each triangle; from wider end, roll up pastry. Brush egg on top of each roll. Preheat the air fryer to 192°C. Air fry rolls in batches, 3 or 4 at a time, 8 minutes per batch, or until pastry is golden brown. Cool on a wire rack; serve while warm or at room temperature.

Lemon Curd Pavlova

Prep time: 10 minutes | Cook time: 1 hour | Serves 4

Shell:	100 g powdered sweetener
3 large egg whites	120 ml lemon juice
¼ teaspoon cream of tartar	4 large eggs
75 g powdered sweetener	120 ml coconut oil
1 teaspoon grated lemon zest	For Garnish (Optional):
1 teaspoon lemon extract	Blueberries
Lemon Curd:	powdered sweetener

Preheat the air fryer to 135°C. Thoroughly grease a pie pan with butter or coconut oil. Make the shell: In a small bowl, use a hand mixer to beat the egg whites and cream of tartar until soft peaks form. With the mixer on low, slowly sprinkle in the sweetener and mix until it's completely incorporated. Add the lemon zest and lemon extract and continue to beat with the hand mixer until stiff peaks form. Spoon the mixture into the greased pie pan, then smooth it across the bottom, up the sides, and onto the rim to form a shell. Bake for 1 hour, then turn off the air fryer and let the shell stand in the air fryer for 20 minutes. (The shell can be made up to 3 days ahead and stored in an airtight container in the refrigerator, if desired.) While the shell bakes, make the lemon curd: In a medium-sized heavy-bottomed saucepan, whisk together the sweetener, lemon juice, and eggs. Add the coconut oil and place the pan on the stovetop over medium heat. Once the oil is melted, whisk constantly until the mixture thickens and thickly coats the back of a spoon, about 10 minutes. Do not allow the mixture to come to a boil. Pour the lemon curd mixture through a fine-mesh strainer into a medium-sized bowl. Place the bowl inside a larger bowl filled with ice water and whisk occasionally until the curd is completely cool, about 15 minutes. Place the lemon curd on top of the shell and garnish with blueberries and powdered sweetener, if desired. Store leftovers in the refrigerator for up to 4 days.

Lime Bars

Prep time: 10 minutes | Cook time: 33 minutes | Makes 12 bars

140 g blanched finely ground almond flour, divided	4 tablespoons salted butter, melted
75 g powdered sweetener, divided	120 ml fresh lime juice
	2 large eggs, whisked

In a medium bowl, mix together 110 g flour, 25 g sweetener, and butter. Press mixture into bottom of an ungreased round nonstick cake pan. Place pan into air fryer basket. Adjust the temperature to 148°C and bake for 13 minutes. Crust will be brown and set in the middle when done. Allow to cool in pan 10 minutes. In a medium bowl, combine remaining flour, remaining sweetener, lime juice, and eggs. Pour mixture over cooled crust and return to air fryer for 20 minutes. Top will be browned and firm when done. Let cool completely in pan, about 30 minutes, then chill covered in the refrigerator 1 hour. Serve chilled.

Almond-Roasted Pears

Prep time: 10 minutes | Cook time: 15 to 20 minutes | Serves 4

Yogurt Topping:	2 whole pears
140-170 g pot vanilla Greek yogurt	4 crushed Biscoff biscuits
¼ teaspoon almond flavoring	1 tablespoon flaked almonds
	1 tablespoon unsalted butter

Stir the almond flavoring into yogurt and set aside while preparing pears. Halve each pear and spoon out the core. Place pear halves in air fryer basket, skin side down. Stir together the crushed biscuits and almonds. Place a quarter of this mixture into the hollow of each pear half. Cut butter into 4 pieces and place one piece on top of biscuit mixture in each pear. Roast at 184°C for 15 to 20 minutes, or until pears have cooked through but are still slightly firm. Serve pears warm with a dollop of yogurt topping.

Crustless Peanut Butter Cheesecake

Prep time: 10 minutes | Cook time: 10 minutes | Serves 2

110 g cream cheese, softened
2 tablespoons powdered sweetener
1 tablespoon all-natural, no-

sugar-added peanut butter
½ teaspoon vanilla extract
1 large egg, whisked

In a medium bowl, mix cream cheese and sweetener until smooth. Add peanut butter and vanilla, mixing until smooth. Add egg and stir just until combined. Spoon mixture into an ungreased springform pan and place into air fryer basket. Adjust the temperature to 148°C and bake for 10 minutes. Edges will be firm, but center will be mostly set with only a small amount of jiggle when done. Let pan cool at room temperature 30 minutes, cover with plastic wrap, then place into refrigerator at least 2 hours. Serve chilled.

Apple Wedges with Apricots

Prep time: 5 minutes | Cook time: 15 to 18 minutes | Serves 4

4 large apples, peeled and sliced into 8 wedges
2 tablespoons light olive oil
95 g dried apricots, chopped

1 to 2 tablespoons granulated sugar
½ teaspoon ground cinnamon

Preheat the air fryer to 180°C. Toss the apple wedges with the olive oil in a mixing bowl until well coated. Place the apple wedges in the air fryer basket and air fry for 12 to 15 minutes. Sprinkle with the dried apricots and air fry for another 3 minutes. Meanwhile, thoroughly combine the sugar and cinnamon in a small bowl. Remove the apple wedges from the basket to a plate. Serve sprinkled with the sugar mixture.

Molten Chocolate Almond Cakes

Prep time: 5 minutes | Cook time: 13 minutes | Serves 3

Butter and flour for the ramekins
110 g bittersweet chocolate, chopped
110 gunsalted butter
2 eggs
2 egg yolks
50 g granulated sugar
½ teaspoon pure vanilla extract, or almond extract

1 tablespoon plain flour
3 tablespoons ground almonds
8 to 12 semisweet chocolate discs (or 4 chunks of chocolate)
Cocoa powder or icing sugar, for dusting
Toasted almonds, coarsely chopped

Butter and flour three (170 g) ramekins. (Butter the ramekins and then coat the butter with flour by shaking it around in the ramekin and dumping out any excess.) Melt the chocolate and butter together, either in the microwave or in a double boiler. In a separate bowl, beat the eggs, egg yolks and sugar together until light and smooth. Add the vanilla extract. Whisk the chocolate mixture into the egg mixture. Stir in the flour and ground almonds. Preheat the air fryer to 164°C. Transfer the batter carefully to the buttered ramekins, filling halfway. Place two or three chocolate discs in the center of the batter and then fill the ramekins to ½-inch below the top with the remaining batter. Place the ramekins into the air fryer basket and air fry for 13 minutes. The sides of the cake should be set, but the centers should be slightly soft. Remove the ramekins from the air fryer and let the cakes sit for 5 minutes. (If you'd like the cake a little less molten, air fry for 14 minutes and let the cakes sit for 4 minutes.) Run a butter knife around the edge of the ramekins and invert the cakes onto a plate. Lift the ramekin off the plate slowly and carefully so that the cake doesn't break. Dust with cocoa powder or icing sugar and serve with a scoop of ice cream and some coarsely chopped toasted almonds.

Pecan Clusters

Prep time: 10 minutes | Cook time: 8 minutes | Serves 8

85 g whole shelled pecans
1 tablespoon salted butter, melted

2 teaspoons powdered sweetener
½ teaspoon ground cinnamon
½ cup low-carb chocolate chips

In a medium bowl, toss pecans with butter, then sprinkle with sweetener and cinnamon. Place pecans into ungreased air fryer basket. Adjust the temperature to 176°C and air fry for 8 minutes, shaking the basket two times during cooking. They will feel soft initially but get crunchy as they cool. Line a large baking sheet with baking paper. Place chocolate in a medium microwave-safe bowl. Microwave on high, heating in 20-second increments and stirring until melted. Place 1 teaspoon chocolate in a rounded mound on ungreased baking paper-lined baking sheet, then press 1 pecan into top, repeating with remaining chocolate and pecans. Place baking sheet into refrigerator to cool at least 30 minutes. Once cooled, store clusters in a large, sealed container in refrigerator up to 5 days.

Cream Cheese Shortbread Cookies

Prep time: 30 minutes | Cook time: 20 minutes | Makes 12 cookies

60 ml coconut oil, melted
55 g cream cheese, softened
100 g granulated sweetener
1 large egg, whisked

190 g blanched finely ground almond flour
1 teaspoon almond extract

Combine all ingredients in a large bowl to form a firm ball. Place dough on a sheet of plastic wrap and roll into a 12-inch-long log shape. Roll log in plastic wrap and place in refrigerator 30 minutes to chill. Remove log from plastic and slice into twelve equal cookies. Cut two sheets of baking paper to fit air fryer basket. Place six cookies on each ungreased sheet. Place one sheet with cookies into air fryer basket. Adjust the temperature to 160°C and bake for 10 minutes, turning cookies halfway through cooking. They will be lightly golden when done. Repeat with remaining cookies. Let cool 15 minutes before serving to avoid crumbling.

Orange, Anise & Ginger Skillet Cookie

Prep time: 20 minutes | Cook time: 15 minutes | Serves 2 to 4

Cookie:
Vegetable oil
125 g plain flour, plus 2 tablespoons
1 tablespoon grated orange zest
1 teaspoon ground ginger
1 teaspoon aniseeds, crushed
¼ teaspoon kosher, or coarse sea salt
4 tablespoons unsalted butter, at room temperature
100 g granulated sugar, plus more for sprinkling
3 tablespoons black treacle
1 large egg
Icing:
60 g icing sugar
2 to 3 teaspoons milk

For the cookie: Generously grease a baking pan with vegetable oil. In a medium bowl, whisk together the flour, orange zest, ginger, aniseeds, and salt. In a medium bowl using a hand mixer, beat the butter and sugar on medium-high speed until well combined, about 2 minutes. Add the treacle and egg and beat until light in color, about 2 minutes. Add the flour mixture and mix on low until just combined. Use a rubber spatula to scrape the dough into the prepared pan, spreading it to the edges and smoothing the top. Sprinkle with sugar. Place the pan in the basket. Set the air fryer to 164°C and bake for 15 minutes, or until sides are browned but the center is still quite soft. Let cool in the pan on a wire rack for 15 minutes. Turn the cookie out of the pan onto the rack. For the icing: Whisk together the sugar and 2 teaspoons of milk. Add 1 teaspoon milk if needed for the desired consistency. Spread, or drizzle onto the cookie.

Lemon Poppy Seed Macaroons

Prep time: 10 minutes | Cook time: 14 minutes | Makes 1 dozen

cookies
2 large egg whites, room temperature
35 g powdered sweetener
2 tablespoons grated lemon zest, plus more for garnish if desired
2 teaspoons poppy seeds
1 teaspoon lemon extract
¼ teaspoon fine sea salt
190 g desiccated unsweetened coconut
Lemon Icing:
25 g sweetener
1 tablespoon lemon juice

Preheat the air fryer to 164°C. Line a pie pan or a casserole dish that will fit inside your air fryer with baking paper. Place the egg whites in a medium-sized bowl and use a hand mixer on high to beat the whites until stiff peaks form. Add the sweetener, lemon zest, poppy seeds, lemon extract, and salt. Mix on low until combined. Gently fold in the coconut with a rubber spatula. Use a 1-inch cookie scoop to place the cookies on the baking paper, spacing them about ¼ inch apart. Place the pan in the air fryer and bake for 12 to 14 minutes, until the cookies are golden, and a toothpick inserted into the center comes out clean. While the cookies bake, make the lemon icing: Place the sweetener in a small bowl. Add the lemon juice and stir well. If the icing is too thin, add a little more sweetener. If the icing is too thick, add a little more lemon juice. Remove the cookies from the air fryer and allow to cool for about 10 minutes, then drizzle with the icing. Garnish with lemon zest, if desired. Store leftovers in an airtight container in the fridge for up to 5 days or in the freezer for up to a month.

Strawberry Pastry Rolls

Prep time: 20 minutes | Cook time: 5 to 6 minutes per batch | Serves 4

85 g low-fat cream cheese
2 tablespoons plain yogurt
2 teaspoons granulated sugar
¼ teaspoon pure vanilla extract
225 g fresh strawberries
8 sheets filo pastry
Butter-flavored cooking spray
45-90 g dark chocolate chips (optional)

In a medium bowl, combine the cream cheese, yogurt, sugar, and vanilla. Beat with hand mixer at high speed until smooth (about 1 minute). Wash strawberries and destem. Chop enough of them to measure 80 g. Stir into cheese mixture. Preheat the air fryer to 164°C. Filo pastry dries out quickly, so cover your stack of filo sheets with baking paper and then place a damp dish towel on top of that. Remove only one sheet at a time as you work. To create one pastry roll, lay out a single sheet of filo. Spray lightly with butter-flavored spray, top with a second sheet of filo and spray the second sheet lightly. Place a quarter of the filling (about 3 tablespoons) about ½ inch from the edge of one short side. Fold the end of the pastry over the filling and keep rolling a turn or two. Fold in both the left and right sides so that the edges meet in the middle of your roll. Then roll up completely. Spray outside of pastry roll with butter spray. When you have 4 rolls, place them in the air fryer basket, seam side down, leaving some space in between each. Air fry for 5 to 6 minutes, until they turn a delicate golden brown. Repeat step 7 for remaining rolls. Allow pastries to cool to room temperature. 1When ready to serve, slice the remaining strawberries. If desired, melt the chocolate chips in microwave or double boiler. Place 1 pastry on each dessert plate, and top with sliced strawberries. Drizzle melted chocolate over strawberries and onto plate.

Pumpkin Pudding with Vanilla Wafers

Prep time: 10 minutes | Cook time: 12 to 17 minutes | Serves 4

250 g canned no-salt-added pumpkin purée (not pumpkin pie filling)
50 g packed brown sugar
3 tablespoons plain flour
1 egg, whisked
2 tablespoons milk
1 tablespoon unsalted butter, melted
1 teaspoon pure vanilla extract
4 low-fat vanilla, or plain wafers, crumbled
Nonstick cooking spray

Preheat the air fryer to 176°C. Coat a baking pan with nonstick cooking spray. Set aside. Mix the pumpkin purée, brown sugar, flour, whisked egg, milk, melted butter, and vanilla in a medium bowl and whisk to combine. Transfer the mixture to the baking pan. Place the baking pan in the air fryer basket and bake for 12 to 17 minutes until set. Remove the pudding from the basket to a wire rack to cool. Divide the pudding into four bowls and serve with the vanilla wafers sprinkled on top.

Chocolate Chip Cookie Cake

4 tablespoons salted butter, melted
65 g granular brown sweetener
1 large egg
½ teaspoon vanilla extract

110 g blanched finely ground almond flour
½ teaspoon baking powder
40 g low-carb chocolate chips

In a large bowl, whisk together butter, sweetener, egg, and vanilla. Add flour and baking powder and stir until combined. Fold in chocolate chips, then spoon batter into an ungreased round nonstick baking dish. Place dish into air fryer basket. Adjust the temperature to 148°C and set the timer for 15 minutes. When edges are browned, cookie cake will be done. Slice and serve warm.

Chapter 9 Pizzas, Wraps, and Sandwiches

Chapter 9 Pizzas, Wraps, and Sandwiches

Chicken-Lettuce Wraps

Prep time: 15 minutes | Cook time: 12 to 16 minutes | Serves 2 to 4

450 g boneless, skinless chicken thighs, trimmed
1 teaspoon vegetable oil
2 tablespoons lime juice
1 shallot, minced
1 tablespoon fish sauce, plus extra for serving
2 teaspoons packed brown sugar
1 garlic clove, minced
⅛ teaspoon red pepper flakes
1 mango, peeled, pitted, and cut
into ¼-inch pieces
80 ml chopped fresh mint
80 ml chopped fresh coriander
80 ml chopped fresh Thai basil
1 head Bibb or butterhead lettuce, leaves separated (227 g)
60 ml chopped dry-roasted peanuts
2 Bird's eye chillies, stemmed and sliced thin

Preheat the air fryer to 204ºC. Pat the chicken dry with paper towels and rub with oil. Place the chicken in air fryer basket and air fry for 12 to 16 minutes, or until the chicken registers 80ºC, flipping and rotating chicken halfway through cooking. Meanwhile, whisk lime juice, shallot, fish sauce, sugar, garlic, and pepper flakes together in large bowl; set aside. Transfer chicken to cutting board, let cool slightly, then shred into bite-size pieces using 2 forks. Add the shredded chicken, mango, mint, coriander, and basil to bowl with dressing and toss to coat. Serve the chicken in the lettuce leaves, passing peanuts, chillies, and extra fish sauce separately.

Smoky Chicken Parm Sandwiches

Prep time: 10 minutes | Cook time: 11 minutes | Serves 2

2 boneless, skinless chicken breasts (227 g each), sliced horizontally in half and separated into 4 thinner cutlets
Rock salt and freshly ground black pepper, to taste
120 ml plain flour
3 large eggs, lightly beaten
120 ml dried breadcrumbs
1 tablespoon smoked paprika
Cooking spray
120 ml marinara sauce, homemade or store-bought
170 g smoked Mozzarella cheese, grated
2 store-bought soft, sesame-seed hamburger or Italian buns, split

Season the chicken cutlets all over with salt and pepper. Set up three shallow bowls: Place the flour in the first bowl, the eggs in the second, and stir together the breadcrumbs and smoked paprika in the third. Coat the chicken pieces in the flour, then dip fully in the egg. Dredge in the paprika breadcrumbs, then transfer to a wire rack set over a baking sheet and spray both sides liberally with cooking spray. Transfer 2 of the chicken cutlets to the air fryer and air fry at 176ºC until beginning to brown, about 6 minutes. Spread

each cutlet with 2 tablespoons of the marinara sauce and sprinkle with one-quarter of the smoked Mozzarella. Increase the heat to 204ºC and cook until the chicken is cooked through and crisp and the cheese is melted and golden brown, about 5 minutes more. Transfer the cutlets to a plate, stack on top of each other, and place inside a bun. Repeat with the remaining chicken cutlets, marinara, smoked Mozzarella, and bun. Serve the sandwiches warm.

Turkey-Hummus Wraps

Prep time: 10 minutes | Cook time: 3 to 7 minutes per batch | Serves 4

4 large wholemeal wraps
120 ml hummus
16 thin slices deli turkey
8 slices provolone cheese
235 ml fresh baby spinach (or more to taste)

To assemble, place 2 tablespoons of hummus on each wrap and spread to within about a half inch from edges. Top with 4 slices of turkey and 2 slices of provolone. Finish with 60 ml baby spinach or pile on as much as you like. Roll up each wrap. You don't need to fold or seal the ends. Place 2 wraps in air fryer basket, seam side down. Air fry at 182ºC for 3 to 4 minutes to warm filling and melt cheese. If you like, you can continue cooking for 2 or 3 more minutes, until the wrap is slightly crispy. Repeat step 4 to cook remaining wraps.

Korean Flavour Beef and Onion Tacos

Prep time: 1 hour 15 minutes | Cook time: 12 minutes | Serves 6

2 tablespoons gochujang chilli sauce
1 tablespoon soy sauce
2 tablespoons sesame seeds
2 teaspoons minced fresh ginger
2 cloves garlic, minced
2 tablespoons toasted sesame oil
2 teaspoons sugar
½ teaspoon rock salt
680 g thinly sliced braising steak
1 medium red onion, sliced
6 corn tortillas, warmed
60 ml chopped fresh coriander
120 ml kimchi
120 ml chopped spring onions

Combine the gochujang, soy sauce, sesame seeds, ginger, garlic, sesame oil, sugar, and salt in a large bowl. Stir to mix well. Dunk the braising steak in the large bowl. Press to submerge, then wrap the bowl in plastic and refrigerate to marinate for at least 1 hour. Preheat the air fryer to 204ºC. Remove the braising steak from the marinade and transfer to the preheated air fryer basket. Add the onion and air fry for 12 minutes or until well browned. Shake the basket halfway through. Unfold the tortillas on a clean work surface, then divide the fried beef and onion on the tortillas. Spread the coriander, kimchi, and spring onions on top. Serve immediately.

Buffalo Chicken French Bread Pizza

Prep time: 10 minutes | Cook time: 12 minutes | Serves 8

Oil, for spraying
1 loaf French bread, cut in half and split lengthwise
4 tablespoons unsalted butter, melted
475 ml shredded or diced rotisserie chicken
110 g soft white cheese

3 tablespoons buffalo sauce, plus more for serving
2 tablespoons dry ranch seasoning
475 ml shredded Mozzarella cheese
80 ml crumbled blue cheese

Line the air fryer basket with parchment and spray lightly with oil. Brush the cut sides of the bread with the melted butter. Place the bread in the prepared basket. You may need to work in batches, depending on the size of your air fryer. Air fry at 204ºC for 5 to 7 minutes, or until the bread is toasted. In a medium bowl, mix together the chicken, soft white cheese, buffalo sauce, and ranch seasoning. Divide the mixture equally among the toasted bread and spread in an even layer. Top with the Mozzarella cheese and blue cheese and cook for another 3 to 5 minutes, or until the cheese is melted. Let cool for 2 to 3 minutes before cutting into 2-inch slices. Serve with additional buffalo sauce for drizzling.

Mushroom Pitta Pizzas

Prep time: 10 minutes | Cook time: 5 minutes | Serves 4

4 (3-inch) pittas
1 tablespoon olive oil
180 ml pizza sauce
1 (113 g) jar sliced mushrooms, drained

½ teaspoon dried basil
2 spring onions, minced
235 ml grated Mozzarella or provolone cheese
235 ml sliced grape tomatoes

Brush each piece of pitta with oil and top with the pizza sauce. Add the mushrooms and sprinkle with basil and spring onions. Top with the grated cheese. Bake at 182ºC for 3 to 6 minutes or until the cheese is melted and starts to brown. Top with the grape tomatoes and serve immediately.

Mediterranean-Pitta Wraps

Prep time: 5 minutes | Cook time: 14 minutes | Serves 4

450 g mackerel fish fillets
2 tablespoons olive oil
1 tablespoon Mediterranean seasoning mix
½ teaspoon chilli powder

Sea salt and freshly ground black pepper, to taste
60 g feta cheese, crumbled
4 tortillas

Toss the fish fillets with the olive oil; place them in the lightly oiled air fryer basket. Air fry the fish fillets at 204ºC for about 14 minutes, turning them over halfway through the cooking time. Assemble your pittas with the chopped fish and remaining ingredients and serve warm.

Bacon and Pepper Sandwiches

Prep time: 15 minutes | Cook time: 7 minutes | Serves 4

80 ml spicy barbecue sauce
2 tablespoons honey
8 slices precooked bacon, cut into thirds
1 red pepper, sliced

1 yellow pepper, sliced
3 pitta pockets, cut in half
300 ml torn butterhead lettuce leaves
2 tomatoes, sliced

In a small bowl, combine the barbecue sauce and the honey. Brush this mixture lightly onto the bacon slices and the red and yellow pepper slices. Put the peppers into the air fryer basket and air fry at 176ºC for 4 minutes. Then shake the basket, add the bacon, and air fry for 2 minutes or until the bacon is browned and the peppers are tender. Fill the pitta halves with the bacon, peppers, any remaining barbecue sauce, lettuce, and tomatoes, and serve immediately.

Dijon and Balsamic Vinaigrette

Prep time: 5 minutes | Cook time: 0 minutes | Makes 12 tablespoons

6 tablespoons water
4 tablespoons Dijon mustard
4 tablespoons balsamic vinegar
1 teaspoon maple syrup

½ teaspoon pink Himalayan salt
¼ teaspoon freshly ground black pepper

In a bowl, whisk together all the ingredients.

Air Fried Philly Cheesesteaks

Prep time: 20 minutes | Cook time: 20 minutes | Serves 2

340 g boneless rib-eye steak, sliced thinly
½ teaspoon Worcestershire sauce
½ teaspoon soy sauce
Rock salt and ground black pepper, to taste
½ green pepper, stemmed, deseeded, and thinly sliced

½ small onion, halved and thinly sliced
1 tablespoon vegetable oil
2 soft sub rolls, split three-fourths of the way through
1 tablespoon butter, softened
2 slices provolone cheese, halved

Preheat the air fryer to 204ºC. Combine the steak, Worcestershire sauce, soy sauce, salt, and ground black pepper in a large bowl. Toss to coat well. Set aside. Combine the pepper, onion, salt, ground black pepper, and vegetable oil in a separate bowl. Toss to coat the vegetables well. Pour the steak and vegetables in the preheated air fryer. Air fry for 15 minutes or until the steak is browned and vegetables are tender. Transfer them on a plate. Set aside. Brush the sub rolls with butter, then place in the air fryer to toast for 3 minutes or until lightly browned. Transfer the rolls on a clean work surface and divide the steak and vegetable mix in between the rolls. Spread with cheese. Arrange the rolls in the air fryer and air fry for 2 minutes or until the cheese melts. Serve immediately.

Beef and Pepper Fajitas

Prep time: 15 minutes | Cook time: 10 minutes | Serves 4

450 g beef sirloin steak, cut into strips
2 shallots, sliced
1 orange pepper, sliced
1 red pepper, sliced
2 garlic cloves, minced
2 tablespoons Cajun seasoning

1 tablespoon paprika
Salt and ground black pepper, to taste
4 corn tortillas
120 ml shredded Cheddar cheese
Cooking spray

Preheat the air fryer to 182°C and spritz with cooking spray. Combine all the ingredients, except for the tortillas and cheese, in a large bowl. Toss to coat well. Pour the beef and vegetables in the preheated air fryer and spritz with cooking spray. Air fry for 10 minutes or until the meat is browned and the vegetables are soft and lightly wilted. Shake the basket halfway through. Unfold the tortillas on a clean work surface and spread the cooked beef and vegetables on top. Scatter with cheese and fold to serve.

Apple Cider Dressing

Prep time: 5 minutes | Cook time: 0 minutes | Serves 2

2 tablespoons apple cider vinegar
⅓ lemon, juiced

⅓ lemon, zested
Salt and freshly ground black pepper, to taste

In a jar, combine the vinegar, lemon juice, and zest. Season with salt and pepper, cover, and shake well.

Cabbage and Mushroom Spring Rolls

Prep time: 20 minutes | Cook time: 35 minutes | Makes 14 spring rolls

2 tablespoons vegetable oil
1 L sliced Chinese leaf
142 g shiitake mushrooms, diced
3 carrots, cut into thin matchsticks
1 tablespoon minced fresh ginger
1 tablespoon minced garlic

1 bunch spring onions, white and light green parts only, sliced
2 tablespoons soy sauce
1 (113 g) package cellophane noodles or vermicelli
¼ teaspoon cornflour
1 (340 g) package frozen spring roll wrappers, thawed
Cooking spray

Heat the olive oil in a non-stick skillet over medium-high heat until shimmering. Add the Chinese leaf, mushrooms, and carrots and sauté for 3 minutes or until tender. Add the ginger, garlic, and spring onions and sauté for 1 minutes or until fragrant. Mix in the soy sauce and turn off the heat. Discard any liquid remains in the skillet and allow to cool for a few minutes. Bring a pot of water to a boil, then turn off the heat and pour in the noodles. Let sit for 10 minutes or until the noodles are al dente. Transfer 235 ml of the noodles in the skillet and toss with the cooked vegetables. Reserve the remaining noodles for other use. Dissolve the cornflour in a small dish of water, then place the wrappers on a clean work surface. Dab the edges of the wrappers with cornflour. Scoop up 3 tablespoons of filling in the centre of each wrapper, then fold the corner in front of you over the filling. Tuck the wrapper under the filling, then fold the corners on both sides into the centre. Keep rolling to seal the wrapper. Repeat with remaining wrappers. Preheat the air fryer to 204°C and spritz with cooking spray. Arrange the wrappers in the preheated air fryer and spritz with cooking spray. Air fry in batches for 10 minutes or until golden brown. Flip the wrappers halfway through. Serve immediately.

Avocado and Slaw Tacos

Prep time: 15 minutes | Cook time: 6 minutes | Serves 4

60 ml plain flour
¼ teaspoon salt, plus more as needed
¼ teaspoon ground black pepper
2 large egg whites
300 ml panko breadcrumbs
2 tablespoons olive oil
2 avocados, peeled and halved, cut into ½-inch-thick slices
½ small red cabbage, thinly

sliced
1 deseeded jalapeño, thinly sliced
2 spring onions, thinly sliced
120 ml coriander leaves
60 ml mayonnaise
Juice and zest of 1 lime
4 corn tortillas, warmed
120 ml sour cream
Cooking spray

Preheat the air fryer to 204°C. Spritz the air fryer basket with cooking spray. Pour the flour in a large bowl and sprinkle with salt and black pepper, then stir to mix well. Whisk the egg whites in a separate bowl. Combine the panko with olive oil on a shallow dish. Dredge the avocado slices in the bowl of flour, then into the egg to coat. Shake the excess off, then roll the slices over the panko. Arrange the avocado slices in a single layer in the basket and spritz the cooking spray. Air fry for 6 minutes or until tender and lightly browned. Flip the slices halfway through with tongs. Combine the cabbage, jalapeño, onions, coriander leaves, mayo, lime juice and zest, and a touch of salt in a separate large bowl. Toss to mix well. Unfold the tortillas on a clean work surface, then spread with cabbage slaw and air fried avocados. Top with sour cream and serve.

Pecan Tartar Sauce

Prep time: 10 minutes | Cook time: 10 minutes | Makes 300 ml

4 tablespoons pecans, finely chopped
120 ml sour cream
120 ml mayonnaise
½ teaspoon grated lemon zest
1½ tablespoons freshly

squeezed lemon juice
2½ tablespoons chopped fresh parsley
1 teaspoon paprika
2 tablespoons chopped dill pickle

Preheat the air fryer to 164°C. Spread the pecans in a single layer on a parchment sheet lightly spritzed with oil. Place the pecans in the air fryer. Air fry for 7 to 10 minutes, stirring every 2 minutes. Let cool. In a medium bowl, mix the sour cream, mayonnaise, lemon zest, and lemon juice until blended. Stir in the parsley paprika, dill pickle, and pecans. Cover and refrigerate to chill for at least 1 hour to blend the flavours. This sauce should be used within 2 weeks.

Orange Dijon Dressing

Prep time: 5 minutes | Cook time: 0 minutes | Serves 2

60 ml extra-virgin olive oil
2 tablespoons freshly squeezed orange juice
1 orange, zested
1 teaspoon garlic powder

¾ teaspoon za'atar seasoning
½ teaspoon salt
¼ teaspoon Dijon mustard
Freshly ground black pepper, to taste

In a jar, combine the olive oil, orange juice and zest, garlic powder, za'atar, salt, and mustard. Season with pepper and shake vigorously until completely mixed.

Cashew Mayo

Prep time: 5 minutes | Cook time: 0 minutes | Makes 18 tablespoons

235 ml cashews, soaked in hot water for at least 1 hour
60 ml plus 3 tablespoons milk
1 tablespoon apple cider vinegar
1 tablespoon freshly squeezed

lemon juice
1 tablespoon Dijon mustard
1 tablespoon aquafaba or egg alternative
⅛ teaspoon pink Himalayan salt

In a food processor, combine all the ingredients and blend until creamy and smooth.

Blue Cheese Dressing

Prep time: 5 minutes | Cook time: 0 minutes | Serves 12

180 ml sugar-free mayonnaise
60 ml sour cream
120 ml double cream
1 teaspoon minced garlic
1 tablespoon freshly squeezed lemon juice

1 tablespoon apple cider vinegar
1 teaspoon hot sauce
½ teaspoon sea salt
110 g blue cheese, crumbled (about 180 ml)

In a medium bowl, whisk together the mayonnaise, sour cream, and double cream. Stir in the garlic, lemon juice, apple cider vinegar, hot sauce, and sea salt. Add the blue cheese crumbles and stir until well combined. Transfer to an airtight container and refrigerate for up to 1 week.

Hot Honey Mustard Dip

Prep time: 5 minutes | Cook time: 0 minutes | Makes 315 ml

180 ml mayonnaise
80 ml spicy brown mustard

60 ml honey
½ teaspoon cayenne pepper

In a medium bowl, stir together the mayonnaise, mustard, and honey until blended. Stir in the cayenne. Cover and chill for 3 hours so the flavours blend. Keep refrigerated in an airtight container for up to 3 weeks.

Miso-Ginger Dressing

Prep time: 10 minutes | Cook time: 0 minutes | Serves 4

1 tablespoon unseasoned rice vinegar or white wine vinegar
1 tablespoon red or white miso
1 teaspoon grated fresh ginger

1 garlic clove, minced
3 tablespoons extra-virgin olive oil

In a small bowl, combine the vinegar and miso into a paste. Add the ginger and garlic and mix well. While whisking, drizzle in the olive oil. Store in the refrigerator in an airtight container for up to 1 week.

Air Fryer Tahini Dressing

Prep time: 5 minutes | Cook time: 0 minutes | Serves 8 to 10

120 ml tahini
60 ml freshly squeezed lemon juice (about 2 to 3 lemons)
60 ml extra-virgin olive oil

1 garlic clove, finely minced or ½ teaspoon garlic powder
2 teaspoons salt

In a glass mason jar with a lid, combine the tahini, lemon juice, olive oil, garlic, and salt. Cover and shake well until combined and creamy. Store in the refrigerator for up to 2 weeks.

Lemony Tahini

Prep time: 5 minutes | Cook time: 0 minutes | Serves 4

180 ml water
120 ml tahini
3 garlic cloves, minced

Juice of 3 lemons
½ teaspoon pink Himalayan salt

In a bowl, whisk together all the ingredients until mixed well.

Vegan Lentil Dip

Prep time: 10 minutes | Cook time: 15 minutes | Makes 700 ml

600 ml water, divided
235 ml dried green or brown lentils, rinsed
80 ml tahini

1 garlic clove
½ teaspoon salt, plus additional as needed

Mix 475 ml water and lentils in a medium pot and bring to a boil over high heat. Once it starts to boil, reduce the heat to low, and bring to a simmer for 15 minutes, or until the lentils are tender. If there is any water remaining in the pot, simply drain it off. Transfer the cooked lentils to a food processor, along with the remaining ingredients. Pulse until a hummus-like consistency is achieved. Taste and add additional salt as needed. It's tasty used as a sandwich spread, and you can also serve it over wholemeal pitta bread or crackers.

Bacon Garlic Pizza

Prep time: 10 minutes | Cook time: 20 minutes | Serves 4

Flour, for dusting
Non-stick baking spray with flour
4 frozen large wholemeal bread rolls, thawed
5 cloves garlic, minced
180 ml pizza sauce

½ teaspoon dried oregano
½ teaspoon garlic salt
8 slices precooked bacon, cut into 1-inch pieces
300 ml shredded Cheddar cheese

On a lightly floured surface, press out each bread roll to a 5-by-3-inch oval. Spray four 6-by-4-inch pieces of heavy-duty foil with non-stick spray and place one crust on each piece. Bake, two at a time, at 188°C for 2 minutes or until the crusts are set, but not browned. Meanwhile, in a small bowl, combine the garlic, pizza sauce, oregano, and garlic salt. When the pizza crusts are set, spread each with some of the sauce. Top with the bacon pieces and Cheddar cheese. Bake, two at a time, for another 8 minutes or until the crust is browned and the cheese is melted and starting to brown.

Air Fryer Avocado Dressing

Prep time: 5 minutes | Cook time: 0 minutes | Makes 12 tablespoons

1 large avocado, pitted and peeled
120 ml water
2 tablespoons tahini
2 tablespoons freshly squeezed lemon juice

1 teaspoon dried basil
1 teaspoon white wine vinegar
1 garlic clove
¼ teaspoon pink Himalayan salt
¼ teaspoon freshly ground black pepper

Combine all the ingredients in a food processor and blend until smooth.

Vegetable Pitta Sandwiches

Prep time: 15 minutes | Cook time: 9 to 12 minutes | Serves 4

1 baby aubergine, peeled and chopped
1 red pepper, sliced
120 ml diced red onion
120 ml shredded carrot

1 teaspoon olive oil
80 ml low-fat Greek yoghurt
½ teaspoon dried tarragon
2 low-salt wholemeal pitta breads, halved crosswise

In a baking pan, stir together the aubergine, red pepper, red onion, carrot, and olive oil. Put the vegetable mixture into the air fryer basket and roast at 200°C for 7 to 9 minutes, stirring once, until the vegetables are tender. Drain if necessary. In a small bowl, thoroughly mix the yoghurt and tarragon until well combined. Stir the yoghurt mixture into the vegetables. Stuff one-fourth of this mixture into each pitta pocket. Place the sandwiches in the air fryer and cook for 2 to 3 minutes, or until the bread is toasted. Serve immediately.

Nugget and Veggie Taco Wraps

Prep time: 5 minutes | Cook time: 15 minutes | Serves 4

1 tablespoon water
4 pieces commercial vegan nuggets, chopped
1 small brown onion, diced

1 small red pepper, chopped
2 cobs grilled corn kernels
4 large corn tortillas
Mixed greens, for garnish

Preheat the air fryer to 204°C. Over a medium heat, sauté the nuggets in the water with the onion, corn kernels and pepper in a skillet, then remove from the heat. Fill the tortillas with the nuggets and vegetables and fold them up. Transfer to the inside of the fryer and air fry for 15 minutes. Once crispy, serve immediately, garnished with the mixed greens.
Chapter 10 Staples, Sauces, Dips, and Dressings

Italian Dressing

Prep time: 5 minutes | Cook time: 0 minutes | Serves 12

60 ml red wine vinegar
120 ml extra-virgin olive oil
¼ teaspoon salt
¼ teaspoon freshly ground black pepper

1 teaspoon dried Italian seasoning
1 teaspoon Dijon mustard
1 garlic clove, minced

In a small jar, combine the vinegar, olive oil, salt, pepper, Italian seasoning, mustard, and garlic. Close with a tight-fitting lid and shake vigorously for 1 minute. Refrigerate for up to 1 week.

Portobello Pizzas

Prep time: 10 minutes | Cook time: 10 minutes | Serves 4

Olive oil
4 large portobello mushroom caps, cleaned and stems removed
Garlic powder

8 tablespoons pizza sauce
16 slices turkey pepperoni
8 tablespoons Mozzarella cheese

Spray the air fryer basket lightly with olive oil. Lightly spray the outside of the mushrooms with olive oil and sprinkle with a little garlic powder, to taste. Turn the mushroom over and lightly spray the sides and top edges of the mushroom with olive oil and sprinkle with garlic powder, to taste. Place the mushrooms in the air fryer basket in a single layer with the top side down. Leave room between the mushrooms. You may need to cook them in batches. Air fry at 176°C for 5 minutes. Spoon 2 tablespoons of pizza sauce on each mushroom. Top each with 4 slices of turkey pepperoni and sprinkle with 2 tablespoons of Mozzarella cheese. Press the pepperoni and cheese down into the pizza sauce to help prevent it from flying around inside the air fryer. Air fry until the cheese is melted and lightly browned on top, another 3 to 5 minutes.

Hemp Dressing

Prep time: 5 minutes | Cook time: 0 minutes | Makes 12 tablespoons

120 ml white wine vinegar
60 ml tahini
60 ml water
1 tablespoon hemp seeds
½ tablespoon freshly squeezed lemon juice
1 teaspoon garlic powder
1 teaspoon dried oregano
1 teaspoon dried basil
1 teaspoon red pepper flakes
½ teaspoon onion powder
½ teaspoon pink Himalayan salt
½ teaspoon freshly ground black pepper

In a bowl, combine all the ingredients and whisk until mixed well.

Chicken and Pickles Sandwich

Prep time: 30 minutes | Cook time: 25 minutes | Serves 4

2 (113 g) boneless, skinless chicken breasts
235 ml dill pickle juice
235 ml milk, divided
Cooking oil
1 egg
120 ml plain flour
Salt and pepper, to taste
4 buns
Pickles

With your knife blade parallel to the cutting board, slice the chicken breasts in half horizontally to create 4 thin cutlets. Place the chicken in a large bowl. Add the pickle juice and 120 ml of milk and toss to coat. Allow the chicken to marinate in the refrigerator for at least 30 minutes. Spray the air fryer basket with cooking oil. In a bowl large enough to dip a chicken cutlet, beat the egg and add the remaining 120 ml of milk. Stir to combine. In another bowl, place the flour and season with salt and pepper. When done marinating, dip each chicken cutlet in the egg and milk mixture and then the flour. Place 2 chicken cutlets in the air fryer. Spray them with cooking oil. Air fry at 370°F for 6 minutes. Open the air fryer and flip the chicken. Cook for an additional 6 minutes. Remove the cooked chicken from the air fryer, then repeat steps 7 and 8 for the remaining 2 chicken cutlets. Serve on buns with pickles.

Air Fryer Artichoke Dip

Prep time: 15 minutes | Cook time: 0 minutes | Serves 3

1 (400 g) can artichoke hearts, drained
450 g goat cheese
2 tablespoons extra-virgin olive oil
2 teaspoons lemon juice
1 garlic clove, minced
1 tablespoon chopped parsley
1 tablespoon chopped chives
½ tablespoon chopped basil
½ teaspoon sea salt
½ teaspoon freshly ground black pepper
Dash of cayenne pepper (optional)
120 ml freshly grated Pecorino Romano

In a food processor, combine all the ingredients, except the Pecorino Romano, and process until well incorporated and creamy. Top with the freshly grated Pecorino Romano. Store in an airtight container in the refrigerator for up to 3 days.

Shrimp and Courgette Curry Potstickers

Prep time: 35 minutes | Cook time: 15 minutes | Serves 10

230 g peeled and deveined shrimp, finely chopped
1 medium courgette, coarsely grated
1 tablespoon fish sauce
1 tablespoon green curry paste
2 spring onions, thinly sliced
60 ml basil, chopped
30 round dumpling wrappers
Cooking spray

Combine the chopped shrimp, courgette, fish sauce, curry paste, spring onions, and basil in a large bowl. Stir to mix well. Unfold the dumpling wrappers on a clean work surface, dab a little water around the edges of each wrapper, then scoop up 1 teaspoon of filling in the middle of each wrapper. Make the potstickers: Fold the wrappers in half and press the edges to seal. Preheat the air fryer to 176°C. Spritz the air fryer basket with cooking spray. Transfer 10 potstickers in the basket each time and spritz with cooking spray. Air fry for 5 minutes or until the potstickers are crunchy and lightly browned. Flip the potstickers halfway through. Repeat with remaining potstickers. Serve immediately.

Mexican Pizza

Prep time: 10 minutes | Cook time: 7 to 9 minutes | Serves 4

180 ml refried beans
120 ml salsa
10 frozen precooked beef meatballs, thawed and sliced
1 jalapeño pepper, sliced
4 wholemeal pitta breads
235 ml shredded pepper Jack or Monterey Jack cheese
120 ml shredded Colby or Gouda cheese
80 ml sour cream

In a medium bowl, combine the refried beans, salsa, meatballs, and jalapeño pepper. Preheat the air fryer for 3 to 4 minutes or until hot. Top the pittas with the refried bean mixture and sprinkle with the cheeses. Bake at 188°C for 7 to 9 minutes or until the pizza is crisp and the cheese is melted and starts to brown. Top each pizza with a dollop of sour cream and serve warm.

Shrimp and Grilled Cheese Sandwiches

Prep time: 10 minutes | Cook time: 5 minutes | Serves 4

300 ml shredded Colby, Cheddar, or Havarti cheese
1 (170 g) can tiny shrimp, drained
3 tablespoons mayonnaise
2 tablespoons minced spring onion
4 slices wholemeal or wholemeal bread
2 tablespoons softened butter

In a medium bowl, combine the cheese, shrimp, mayonnaise, and spring onion, and mix well. Spread this mixture on two of the slices of bread. Top with the other slices of bread to make two sandwiches. Spread the sandwiches lightly with butter. Air fry at 204°C for 5 to 7 minutes or until the bread is browned and crisp and the cheese is melted. Cut in half and serve warm.

Printed in Great Britain
by Amazon

15294032R00045